Institute of Leadership
& Management

super series

Solving
Problems and
Making
Decisions

FIFTH EDITION

Published for the
Institute of Leadership & Management

ELSEVIER

AMSTERDAM • BOSTON • HEIDELBERG • LONDON • NEW YORK • OXFORD
PARIS • SAN DIEGO • SAN FRANCISCO • SINGAPORE • SYDNEY • TOKYO
Pergamon Flexible Learning is an imprint of Elsevier

Pergamon
Flexible
Learning

Pergamon Flexible Learning
An imprint of Elsevier
The Boulevard, Langford Lane, Kidlington, Oxford, OX5 1GB
30 Corporate Drive, Burlington, MA 01803

First published 1986
Second edition 1991
Third edition 1997
Fourth edition 2003
Fifth edition 2007
Reprinted 2008, 2009

Editor: David Pardey

Based on material in previous editions of this work

The views expressed in this work are those of the authors and do not
necessarily reflect those of the Institute of Leadership & Management
or of the Publisher.

Notice
No responsibility is assumed by the publisher for any injury and/or damage to persons
or property as a matter of products liability, negligence or otherwise, or from any use
or operation of any methods, products, instructions or ideas contained in the material
herein.

British Library Cataloguing in Publication Data
A catalogue record for this book is available from the British Library

ISBN: 978-0-08-046423-7

For information on Pergamon Flexible Learning
visit our website at www.elsevierdirect.com

Institute of Leadership & Management
Registered office
1 Giltspur Street
London
EC1A 9DD
Telephone 020 7294 2470
www.i-l-m.com
ILM is a subsidiary of the City & Guilds Group

Working together to grow
libraries in developing countries

www.elsevier.com | www.bookaid.org | www.sabre.org

ELSEVIER   BOOK AID International   Sabre Foundation

Printed and bound in *Great Britain*

09 10 11 12   12 11 10 9 8 7 6 5 4 3

Contents

Contents

Series preface

Whether you are a tutor/trainer or studying management development to further your career, Super Series provides an exciting and flexible resource to help you to achieve your goals. The fifth edition is completely new and up-to-date, and has been structured to perfectly match the Institute of Leadership & Management (ILM)'s new unit-based qualifications for first line managers. It also harmonizes with the 2004 national occupational standards in management and leadership, providing an invaluable resource for S/NVQs at Level 3 in Management.

Super Series is equally valuable for anyone tutoring or studying any management programmes at this level, whether leading to a qualification or not. Individual workbooks also support short programmes, which may be recognized by ILM as Endorsed or Development Awards, or provide the ideal way to undertake CPD activities.

For learners, coping with all the pressures of today's world, Super Series offers you the flexibility to study at your own pace to fit around your professional and other commitments. You don't need a PC or to attend classes at a specific time – choose when and where to study to suit yourself! And you will always have the complete workbook as a quick reference just when you need it.

For tutors/trainers, Super Series provides an invaluable guide to what needs to be covered, and in what depth. It also allows learners who miss occasional sessions to 'catch up' by dipping into the series.

Super Series provides unrivalled support for all those involved in first line management and supervision.

Unit specification

Title:	Solving problems and making decisions	Unit Ref:	M3.01
Level:	3		
Credit value:	2		

Learning outcomes *The learner* will		Assessment criteria *The learner* can *(in an organization with which the learner is familiar)*
1. Know how to describe a problem, its nature, scope and impact	1.1	Describe a problem, its nature scope and impact
2. Know how to gather and interpret information to solve a problem	2.1	Gather and interpret information to identify possible solutions to a problem
3. Know how to solve a problem	3.1 3.2	Briefly summarize the options, providing facts and evidence, not just opinion Use at least *one* simple decision-making technique to evaluate options to arrive at the best solution
4. Know how to plan the implementation and communication of decisions	4.1 4.2	Plan the implementation and communication of the decision Briefly discuss which monitoring and review techniques could be used to evaluate outcomes

Workbook introduction

1 ILM Super Series 4 study links

This workbook addresses the issues of *Solving Problems and Making Decisions*. Should you wish to extend your study to other Super Series workbooks covering related or different subject areas, you will find a comprehensive list at the back of this book.

2 Links to ILM qualifications

This workbook relates to the learning outcomes of Unit M3.15 Solving Problems & Making Decisions from the ILM Level 3 Award, Certificate and Diploma in First Line Management.

3 Links to S/NVQs in management

This workbook relates to the following Unit of the Management Standards which are used in S/NVQs in Management, as well as a range of other S/NVQs:

C6. Implementing change
F6. Monitor and solve customer service problems

4 Workbook objectives

We all encounter problems in every sphere of our lives, but in a management context they are particularly important. In fact, it's often claimed that the most important things that managers have to do are to solve problems and make decisions.

Problem solving and decision making are closely connected. Choosing a solution, for example (the subject of Session C in this workbook), is basically about **deciding** which possible solution to adopt.

Nevertheless, there is a distinction between problem solving and decision making. Problem solving involves exploration and analysis to gather information. Decision making involves using that information to enable decisions to be made that are likely to achieve the goals of the problem-solving process. In this sense, decision making is part of problem solving, and so is integrated into the process.

Some problems are quite easy to deal with but, unfortunately, a lot of the problems that you and other managers, supervisors and team leaders will face are anything but clear-cut. Often you will find that in addition to being difficult to solve:

- problems are hard to pin down and describe clearly
- the causes are obscure
- there are several possible solutions, and it's unclear which would be best
- the best solutions seem difficult to put into effect.

Fortunately, if we adopt a careful and systematic approach, there are few problems that cannot be tackled successfully. In the four workbook sessions that follow you will be taken through a six-stage process for solving problems:

- **recognize** the problem
- accept **ownership** of the problem
- **understand** the problem
- **choose** the best solution
- **implement** the solution
- monitor and **evaluate** the solution.

We will consider how to decide whether problems are our responsibility, and whether they are worth spending time and energy on. We will look at ways of describing and dissecting problems, so that their causes can be pinned down accurately. There will be coverage of practical techniques like brainstorming and problem analysis, and of some approaches to matching causes and solutions. We will also look at various techniques for analysing quantitative and qualitative data to enable you to understand the problem better. Finally, the most important, but perhaps least exciting stage of the process will be addressed – ensuring that your solutions work in practice.

4.1 Objectives

When you have completed this workbook you will be better able to:

- describe and analyse problems;
- identify the cause or causes of problems;
- understand the need to collect information about problems;
- analyse numerical data;
- use statistics to enhance understanding of information;
- analyse qualitative information;
- generate a range of possible solutions and decide which will work best;
- use decision-making models;
- implement your chosen solution and evaluate its effectiveness.

5 Activity planner

You may want to look at the following Activities now, so that you can start collecting material – or do whatever else is required – as soon as possible:

Activity 4 on pages 4–5 asks you to review some problems that you have recently had to deal with. The main aim here is to identify problems that were not foreseen, but could have been, and to understand why this was.

Activity 7 on page 11 is the first in a series of six activities in which you will be asked to analyse a problem that is facing you at work.

Activity 17 on page 26 is designed to give you practice in brainstorming, a key technique in management. You will need to get together with some friends or colleagues in order to do this.

Some or all of these Activities may provide the basis of evidence for your S/NVQ portfolio. All Portfolio Activities and the Work-based assignment are signposted with this icon.

The icon states the elements to which the Portfolio Activities and Work-based assignment relate.

Session A
Problems large and small

1 Introduction

Problems come in all forms, shapes and sizes. The problem in Activity 1 appears to be a simple one.

Activity 1

What would you do if you were offered the choice of:

a   receiving £1 million in one lump sum;
b   getting just one penny on the first day of a month, two on the second day, four on the third, eight pennies on the fourth and so on, to the end of the month?

It may look like a simple choice, but you would be well advised to sit down with pencil and paper and/or calculator, and work out which option is better. You will find the answer on page 128.

This little puzzle illustrates the theme of the first part of the workbook.

It's a good idea to think about the problem before coming up with a solution!

2 What do we mean by 'a problem'?

'Problem' is one of those words we use loosely to describe any situatic which looks uncertain or difficult in any respect. For the purposes of th workbook we need to be more specific about what we mean.

Activity 2

3 mins

Write down in your own words a definition of the word 'problem'.

_____

_____

You might have answered:

- something hard to understand;
- a doubtful or difficult question;
- something difficult to control, which disrupts smooth progress;
- a puzzle or mystery of some kind;
- a task that is difficult to carry out.

All of these would be correct, but the definition on which this workbook based is:

Something which is difficult to deal with or to resolve.

Of course, some problems are more difficult to deal with than others.

In this workbook we will be concerned with those problems which appear t offer no easy solution; especially the kind that makes us feel we don't kno where to begin.

Activity 3 · 5 mins

Think about some problems you've had at work recently. Try to make a list of at least three different **kinds** of problem. You don't need to worry about the details at this stage; just make a note of the general type of problem you seemed to be dealing with (for example, relations between members of the work team).

The list of possible problems at work could be endless; the following are just some suggestions to which many more could be added.

- **Deviation problems:** where something has gone wrong, and **corrective** action is needed. For example:

  - equipment malfunction;
  - supplies not received;
  - illness among the work team;
  - 'log jams' of work or people.

- **Potential problems:** where problems may be arising for the future and **preventive** action is needed. For example:

  - strong rivalries between members of the work team;
  - increased demand which you may have difficulty meeting;
  - growing staff turnover.

- **Improvement problems:** how to be more productive, efficient and responsive in the future. For example:

  - upgrading products, premises, equipment or methods;
  - installing a new system;
  - equipping people with new skills;
  - changing procedures to meet new safety standards.

In this workbook we will look at techniques which you can apply to problems in all sorts of situations.

The first of these techniques, and perhaps the most important of all, is really about an **attitude of mind**. Perhaps you've heard the expression: 'When you are up to your knees in alligators, it's difficult to remember that it's your job to clear the swamp.'

> Detach yourself from the problem. Be objective. Analyse. Stand clear of the alligators!

You probably feel that you are 'up to your knees in alligators' much of the time. It may be as much as you can do to stop yourself being eaten alive by the problems that surround you, let alone solve them. The only thing to do is to 'get out of the swamp'.

2.1 Problems foreseen and unforeseen

'Problems, like accidents, can always be prevented.'

Do you agree with this statement? Or do you believe that, as an individual, you can't always prevent or foresee what happens to you? Perhaps you feel that there are cases where **you** can see problems arising, but you can't convince others that they should be taken seriously?

> While her boss was away, someone asked Ruth, the senior technician, whether the new computers had been ordered. She knew they hadn't, but since her boss had obtained several quotations, she identified the cheapest that met the specification, and placed the order. Of the 11 computers delivered, all but two had faults in the operating software, which, it soon emerged, had been copied illegally by what was in fact a 'rogue' supplier. It didn't occur to Ruth to consider which suppliers were reliable and which weren't. But if her boss had been there, this problem probably wouldn't have arisen.

Activity 4 · 15 mins

S/NVQ
C6 or F6

This Activity may provide the basis of appropriate evidence for your S/NVQ portfolio. If you are intending to take this course of action, it might be better to write your answers on separate sheets of paper.

Think about some problems involving your work that have arisen in recent weeks or months.

Try to identify four altogether: two which you **could not** have foreseen or prevented, and two which you feel **could have** been foreseen and prevented, but which weren't. Write brief details below.

Could not have foreseen or prevented:

1 _____

_____

_____

2 _____

_____

_____

Could have foreseen and prevented:

1 _____

_____

_____

2 _____

_____

_____

Now think again about these problems.

Are you **sure** that the 'unforeseeable' ones really couldn't have been anticipated?

Why was it that the 'foreseeable' ones **weren't** anticipated?

What lessons can you draw from this? What will you personally do differently in future?

You probably thought of several situations where a little more planning and forethought would have prevented a problem from developing. You should always try to ensure that a problem doesn't occur in the first place. Failing this, bear in mind that the chosen solution to a problem should always include plans to prevent the problem happening again.

Being able to anticipate and prevent problems is a basic management skill, so you should try to learn lessons from situations like these. From now on, as you encounter situations which may turn out to be problems, try to 'get your retaliation in early'.

2.2 The six stages of problem solving

There are six stages to the problem-solving process:

- Stage 1: **recognize** the problem

  Until you recognize that a **problem** exists, obviously you won't take any **action**. The **early recognition** of problems in your job is a skill that usually improves with experience. Experience will also tell you where something that might appear worrying can safely be ignored because it's unlikely to turn into a problem.

- Stage 2: accept **ownership** of the problem

  Not all problems that **affect** you are up to you personally to **solve**. If you do not have the authority or ability to solve a problem, it is usually wiser to pass it on to someone who does.

- Stage 3: **understand** the problem

  Once you know you have a problem and have accepted ownership of it, you must **define** it clearly, **find out** all you can about it, and **collect information** that will help you find ways of tackling it. In particular it pays to identify the causes of a problem.

- Stage 4: **choose** the best solution

  As will be emphasized in Session B, there are a number of useful approaches to **analysing** a problem that can lead you to a solution. In Session C we will concentrate on ways to generate new ideas when the problem cannot be solved using the known facts.

- Stage 5: **implement** the solution

  When you believe that you understand the problem, and can see a way of solving it, you can take action. Sometimes, caution is required because you cannot be sure that the plan will work. Sometimes you will have managed to find only a partial solution, and you will need to test this out before attempting to solve the rest of the problem.

- Stage 6: monitor and **evaluate** the solution

  After you've implemented a solution, you need to check whether it has worked, and whether it has had any effects that were not expected. Perhaps most important of all, you need to learn for next time.

  The rest of this workbook looks at each stage in detail. Meanwhile, Activity 5 will get you thinking about the process as a whole.

3 Stage 1: recognize the problem

Stage 1 starts with developing an awareness of possible problems before they hit you.

3.1 Looking out for problems

You may feel you have more than enough to do without looking for problems, but there are some advantages in asking yourself: 'What would happen if …?' or 'Supposing this were not to work …?'.

Activity 5   3 mins

Make a note of two advantages of actively looking out for potential problems.

_____

_____

_____

_____

You are often likely to find that you are trying to cope with more problems than you would like. This shouldn't, however, stop you from looking for more on the horizon. There are two reasons for this.

- The earlier you spot a potential problem, the better you'll be prepared to cope with it.
- When everything is going smoothly, there may be an opportunity to take a fresh look at things that you normally take for granted. You can then use problem-solving techniques to try to find a better way of doing them.

3.2 Is there really a problem?

On the other hand, it's a mistake to go too far in the other direction, and to imagine problems at every turn.

You may well have come across the kind of person who is always finding problems which aren't there. Often it's because of lack of experience, or fear of the unknown, or just a tendency to panic. Asking the question 'Are you sure?' can often save precious time and resources.

Are you sure there really is a problem?

Even when there really is a problem, it may not need a solution. Some problems solve themselves; others can safely be ignored.

Can you ignore it? Can you side-step it?

3.3 Is the problem worth solving?

Sometimes there is a real dilemma in trying to solve a problem, because we can see that its solution may result in further problems.

Desmond is a supervisor in a small family company. Although he enjoys his job very much, the company is not doing well. Desmond's problem is that he would like to earn more money. He goes to his boss and asks for a rise in salary. The boss says that the way that sales are going, this just isn't possible.

Desmond is pretty sure that he could get a job elsewhere for more money. However, he knows that if he does this, he will miss his present job, and the people he works with, very much.

Activity 6 · 5 mins

If you were Desmond, what would you do?

_____

_____

_____

_____

_____

There's no easy answer to this problem, and you may have felt you didn't have enough information. For example, it would help a great deal to know the reason why Desmond needs the extra money. Is it for some luxury, or is he really finding it hard to 'make ends meet'? Also, is Desmond taking other factors into account, such as his future career prospects?

Desmond's case is typical of the difficulties we all face in our lives. We would like neat problems with clear-cut answers, but our experience tells us that there is nearly always a price to be paid for solving a problem. For example, in medicine, tremendous advances have been made using drugs in the treatment of disease. Yet we are told that no successful drug has yet been discovered which does not have some adverse side-effect.

So it is often necessary to question the importance of finding a solution. It's worth asking yourself the following questions:

- Is there a solution to this problem?
- Will solving it be worth the effort?
- What price am I prepared to pay for solving it?

4 Stage 2: accept ownership of the problem

Once you've decided that:

■ a problem exists;
■ and needs solving;
■ and is worth solving;

you then need to ask yourself: **Is the problem really mine?**

If it is, then you must accept ownership of the problem, and take responsibility for solving it. However, you may not get much benefit – or approval – from trying to solve problems that aren't really yours.

> Selim was in charge of outpatients administration in a hospital. Patients often complained to him about the difficulty of parking their cars at the hospital. Selim sympathized, and he encouraged some of them to write to the hospital manager asking for the old tennis courts to be opened up for parking. In fact they sent a copy to the local newspaper, and there was some adverse publicity. The hospital manager was very annoyed to hear that Selim was behind all this, and reprimanded him. 'You are fully at liberty to report problems to me or anyone else,' she told him, 'but meddling in matters that don't concern you must stop.'

> **Sometimes problems are SEPs – someone else's problem!**

When you accept ownership of a problem, this implies that you will:

■ take responsibility for solving it;
■ put your personal energy and authority into doing so;
■ ensure that those concerned know that you are accepting ownership.

Bear in mind, though, that even if you accept ownership of a problem, you are not necessarily on your own. Other people may be able to help you solve the problem, and indeed may have a **responsibility** to do so.

Activity 7

S/NVQs
C6 or F6

This activity is the first in a series of six in which you will use a range of techniques to solve a problem that is currently facing you at work. They could jointly provide the basis of evidence for your S/NVQ portfolio. If you are intending to take this course of action, it might be better to write your answers on separate sheets of paper.

Select a problem that is currently facing you at work. It should be:

■ something important enough to justify spending some time on getting it right;
■ a problem which you 'own' and which you are responsible for solving;
■ difficult or complex enough for the solution not to be obvious from the start.

It could be:

■ a **deviation** problem, where something is not going to plan, and it's not clear why;
■ a **potential** problem, where something is starting to develop that may cause difficulties if it isn't dealt with;
■ an **improvement** problem, where there's a need to find better ways of doing things for the future (for example increased productivity, better safety, or changes to working methods).

Start by making a list of problems that might be suitable, marking them 'deviation', 'potential', or 'improvement'. Take time to think about them before you make your choice.

Now write down the problem you have selected and describe it briefly.

_____

_____

_____

_____

_____

You will be asked to work on analysing and solving this problem at a number of points throughout this workbook, so make sure you have made a suitable choice. Remember that the problem should be **important enough**, and **difficult** or **complex enough**, to be worth working on. It should also be a problem that **you personally** are responsible for solving.

5 Stage 3: understand the problem

We will now move on to deal with stage three of the problem-solving process – **understand the problem**. We will focus primarily on how to understand more complex problems by **defining** them and then **analysing** them in order to find the **possible causes.**

5.1 Define the problem

A problem must be clearly defined before you can expect to solve it. All problems, even simple ones, benefit from being clearly defined and stated, and a good test is:

Can you write it down?

Let's look at an example of a problem which initially lacks definition, and then see how much it helps to define it on paper.

Bill supervises a team that repairs computer assemblies. He confides his problems to a friend over an after-work pint.

'The work just keeps piling up. I have to divide the team's time between repairing rejects sent over from Production and faulty items that are returned by customers. The boss is constantly telling me that this or that customer has complained about slow service, but he won't let us have any more staff. He just says I should get better organized. Production keep sending me more and more rejects, and they're always pressuring us too. Everyone's fed up, I'm fed up, and it's getting harder and harder to face it all.'

Activity 8 ·

7 mins

Briefly define Bill's problem, as he sees it. Try not to make too many assumptions, and don't suggest solutions at this stage.

_____

_____

_____

_____

One way of defining Bill's problem is like this:

■ Bill's team does not seem able to cope with its workload. This is resulting in low staff morale, unhappy customers, and an unhappy boss.

This definition is helpful, but we can improve on it by defining the problem in terms of the **desired outcome**. In practice, this might have more than one side to it.

We will return to this case study – which we'll call **Bill's problem** – repeatedly during the remainder of this workbook.

■ What does Bill want to achieve?
■ What does the company want to achieve?

Activity 9 ·

10 mins

What would you say is the desired outcome to this problem:

a from Bill's point of view?

_____

_____

_____

b from the company's point of view?

_____

_____

_____

13

If we had asked Bill this question, he might have given one of the following answers.

- 'I simply want my team to keep up with the workload. That way everyone will be happy.'

- 'I'd like to prove to my boss, and everyone else, that they need to change the whole way of working around here.'

- 'All I want is a quiet life.'

- 'I want to reduce the amount of work they throw at my team.'

The company, on the other hand, will be concerned with ensuring the best possible mix of efficiency, service quality and productivity.

So while Bill is focusing on 'Why is there too much work?', the company is probably thinking in terms of 'Why isn't Bill delivering the goods?'

These are two very different views of the situation, and they imply that the solution is open to question. Bill wants a reduced workload, but for the company that will not be an acceptable solution.

5.2 Stating the problem clearly

A good starting point is to draw up a 'problem statement'.

Activity 10

6 mins

Use the 'problem statement grid' (below) to identify the key issues in Bill's problem. Tick the right-hand column if you think you need more information before you can answer this question.

Key issues	Need more information
1 Describe the problem briefly:	
2 What effect is it having?	
3 Where is it?	
4 When was it first noticed?	
5 Is there anything special or distinctive about it?	

It is not possible to answer Questions 4 and 5 on the basis of the information we have so far. However, we will come back to these in a moment.

The rest of the questions are fairly easy to answer. The problem is that B
and the repair team are finding it difficult to meet the competing demands
the factory and the customers. This is creating stress among the team ar
damaging morale. It is probably also damaging relations with the customer
**Note that this statement of the problem expresses it from bot
Bill's point of view and that of the company.**

The problem lies in the repair section. (We have no evidence that other par
of the company are overloaded.) However, this does not necessarily mea
that the **cause(s) and solution** also lie in the repair section!

Activity 11

2 mins

Are there any other questions that it might be useful to add to the 'proble
statement'?

_____

_____

_____

_____

_____

_____

In this case I would add three questions, though these wouldn't apply to a
problem statements.

How big is the problem? – You could rate it from, say, 1 to 10 for seriousness

Who ought to be helping to find its cause and solution? In th
example we're working through, I would say that Bill's boss and the productio
manager also ought to be helping, because they have a direct interest in th
outcome.

We can show this in a diagram (a useful and quick technique):

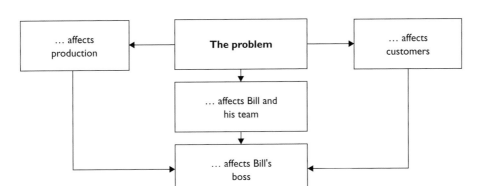

In the end all the pressure focuses on Bill's boss: Bill should be expecting a good deal of help from that direction!

What solutions have already been tried, and what was the outcome? Problems like this tend to drag on over a considerable time, and there may well have been some attempts to sort it out. Knowing what these were, and why they failed (as they presumably did) will save a lot of time when getting down to finding causes and solutions.

5.3 Spotting distinctive features

By identifying when a problem first appeared, and any unusual or distinctive features that it has, you can discover valuable clues about **causes**, which in turn will help find a **solution.**

In a famous case study described by management experts Charles H. Kepner and Benjamin B. Tregoe, a company found that some of its extruded viscose elements were being contaminated with carbon. This was accurately timed as starting at 3.52 a.m. and ceasing at 4.03 a.m. There were four distinctive features about the problem:

- It started and stopped abruptly.
- There was no immediate recurrence of the problem.
- Although four identical machines were operating at the time, only one was affected.
- The machine had a total of 480 nozzles extruding filaments, and the problem affected all of them.

Sherlock Holmes would have been delighted to have such a wonderful set of clues!

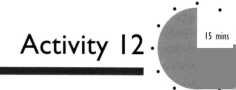

Activity 12

15 mins

S/NVQs C6 or F6

This Activity is the second in a series of six which could jointly provide th basis of evidence for your S/NVQ portfolio. If you are intending to take th course of action, it might be better to write your answers on separate shee of paper.

Use the 'problem statement grid', with extra questions if appropriate, to he define the problem you identified in Activity 7.

Key issues	Need more information
1 Describe the problem briefly:	
2 What effect is it having?	
3 Where is it?	
4 When was it first noticed?	
5 Is there anything special or distinctive about it?	

Remember to be specific in completing the grid. If the problem suddenly began at 4.18 on a Friday afternoon, say so: this may point to the cause being something that happened immediately before 4.18.

5.4 Gathering information

To find the causes of a problem, you must gather information. (You must also gather information when generating possible solutions and establishing what the constraints – the restrictions – on the solution are. We will return to this subject in Session B.) Sometimes information will be available from the out-set, but sometimes you will have to go looking for it. Information will allow you to define the problem precisely.

Activity 13

10 mins

What information have you been given about Bill's problem? List each point separately.

_____

_____

_____

_____

_____

_____

What else do you need to know?

_____

_____

_____

_____

_____

The information that we have about Bill's problem consists of the following:

- Bill's team is responsible for repairing both defective goods rejected from the factory and items returned from customers;
- Repaired goods are not being returned fast enough, either to the factory or to the customers; both have complained about this fact;
- Bill's boss has rejected the idea of increasing staff as a solution to the problem.

The information that we need to know includes when the problem started, and whether there is anything special or distinctive about it.

In fact, although the team always had to work hard, the problem really began to surface in January; it is now March and there has been no improvement. On the other hand the problem doesn't seem to have any unusual or distinctive features.

5.5 How much information?

If you have too little information, you cannot reach a good-quality decision. You need to acquire more information – but how much?

For example, suppose a first line manager named Ronald was trying to decide which of three different specifications for fire extinguishers would be most appropriate for his office, which contained a lot of electrical equipment. He read through the manufacturers' literature but wasn't sure. Did it tell him everything he wanted to know? He called the local Fire Prevention Department for advice. They faxed him some further documents. Still Ronald felt uncertain. He wrote back to the manufacturers asking some technical questions and asked one of his team to search the Internet for any relevant articles.

He contacted the British Standards Institution, the Department of Trade and Industry, the Fire Protection Association and his company's insurers, all of whom sent him more information. Finally, he got hold of some obscure research reports, which he found very hard to understand. In the end, he spent more than two whole days studying the information before he made his decision.

Choosing the right fire extinguishers is an important decision, and it is vital to have reliable information. But, as we have seen, information has a cost to set against its value:

- it may have to be paid for;
- it takes time to locate and acquire;
- it takes time to read and understand.

If Ronald earns £20,000 a year, with additional costs taking his total cost to his employer to around £40,000, that works out at over £160 per working day. If it has taken him more than two days to study the fire extinguisher issue, the cost of his time alone is probably over £320. To this must be added the time of the other team member involved, other colleagues, phone calls, postage, and so on.

Then we have to consider the cost of the things Ronald could have been doing in that time – perhaps more important and valuable tasks.

Was Ronald spending his time cost-effectively?

Like so many things, the cost-value curve for information tends to follow the 80–20 rule, which is to say that 20% of the information provides 80% of the value. In many cases, any extra information collected will merely reinforce and confirm what was learned from the most useful 20%. This is probably the case in Ronald's investigation of fire extinguishers.

This does not usually mean that the first 20% of the information you obtain is the most valuable. The valuable bits may be mixed up with all the rest. So how do you decide which information is worth focusing on?

Managers use information to answer questions and, for them, good-quality information is that which does this quickly, simply, accurately and reliably. This means it must be relevant and thorough, but concise.

6 Analyse the problem

Problem analysis consists of writing down a series of statements that will help locate the problem more precisely. The statements take the form of saying what the problem **is** and what it **could be, but is not** . . . Here's an example of a problem analysis grid relating to the 'carbon on the filaments' case.

The problem is:	The problem could be, but is not:
A short-term one (11 minutes only)	A continuous one
Restricted to one machine	Affecting all four machines
Affecting all nozzles on this machine	Affecting only some of them
One that might recur	One that has immediately recurred
etc.	

This helps to find a cause, and then a solution, by drawing attention to the specific location of the problem – in this case, for just 11 minutes, on all 480 nozzles of just one machine out of four. **Any causes that are suggested must account for this specific pattern of events.**

Activity 14

S/NVQs
C6 or F6

This Activity is the third in a series of six which could jointly provide the basis of evidence for your S/NVQ portfolio.

Analyse the problem you are working on, using the blank problem analysis grid or a separate sheet of paper.

The problem is:	The problem could be, but is not:

Sometimes, completing a problem analysis grid points clearly to the cause of the problem – but not often. The more important the problem is, the more it pays to take time to think.

6.1 Identify possible causes

Before we attempt a solution, we must identify the cause or causes of the problem. This means more Sherlock Holmes work.

Activity 15

More information is needed to establish the causes of Bill's problem. Where would you now concentrate your detective work?

You need to concentrate on the point when the problem began – in January. Before January, there wasn't a problem. From January on, there was. Something must have changed. If we can establish what it was, we'll be a lot nearer a solution.

Activity 16

List some of the things that might have changed in January, and so have possibly given rise to a problem.

Once you start thinking about this, you'll realize that a lot of things may have changed within one or more of the following:

- the work itself;
- the working environment;
- the product;
- management;
- the make-up of the team;
- physical factors.

Sometimes the thing that changed will be obvious (for example, if a highly experienced technician left the team in January and was replaced by someone who is incompetent). Sometimes there are many possibilities, none of them obvious.

The Kepner–Tregoe case study illustrated this point.

EXTENSION 1
The book in which Charles Kepner and Benjamin Tregoe explain how the 'carbon on the filaments' case was solved is a classic of management literature, now published under the title *The New Rational Manager*. See page 124.

> The analysis of the carbon-coated filaments problem clearly showed that something local and temporary had affected all the output nozzles on one specific machine. The investigators looked for sources of carbon. There were none in the factory, but outside there was a rail-yard, where coal-burning steam trains were used at all times of day and night. Could smoke have entered the air-intake of one machine but not the others? The answer proved to be yes. The four machines had separate intakes, many metres apart. It also transpired that on the night in question a steam shunting engine had been left for precisely 11 minutes in a position where its smoke drifted over just one of the four air intakes.
>
> Careful analysis had successfully traced the cause of the problem.

In the filament case, problem analysis showed clearly where the cause must lie. It was then a matter of logical deduction (plus a search for further relevant information) that led to the cause.

Brainstorming is useful in two distinct parts of the problem-solving process – when you're looking for causes and when you're looking for solutions.

However, logical deduction is not always the best route to the cause, especially where the problem is less precise, and there may possibly be many causes.

Often we need to do the opposite of focusing logically, and open up our minds to the widest range of possibilities, as in Bill's case. One technique for doing this is **brainstorming.**

6.2 Brainstorming

The idea of brainstorming is to come up with as complete a list of possibilities as you can, without worrying about whether they are brilliant or lousy, big or small. You can sort that out later.

Brainstorming is about **creativity**, and it's widely used in management for helping to solve problems and make decisions.

It is one of the many situations where two heads are better than one, and four or five are better still. The more different brains are at work, the bigger the storm of ideas.

How to brainstorm for causes of a problem

There are two stages in brainstorming. The first is creative, wide-ranging and should be free from analysis and judgements. Its rules are as follows.

- Everyone who is to take part gathers in a room away from the interruptions of normal work. Six to twelve people is the ideal number.
- A session lasts for a fixed time period: 30 minutes is about right.
- A chair or leader is chosen. His or her job is to define the problem, to remind everyone present of the rules of brainstorming, and generally keep control. Most important, he or she has to stop anyone trying to judge or evaluate the ideas put forward.
- Someone must note down all the ideas that are put forward. In a small group the leader could do this, by writing all ideas on a marker board or flipchart.
- Most important of all: everyone is free to put forward any idea at all, however bizarre or seemingly inappropriate. No one is allowed to say: 'That's no good' or 'I don't see the point of that' or 'That's just nonsense'.
- The idea of the session is to be creative, not logical.
- All ideas are evaluated **after** the session, not during it.
- Anyone who might have useful ideas can take part. It shouldn't be exclusive to 'management' or to people who are normally paid to think about the subject in hand.

When everyone is relaxed and ready, the leader asks for suggestions. Everyone should let their thoughts roam widely.

The leader jots down **everything** that **anyone** mentions that may have the slightest relevance to the issue. (It's best to write the suggestions on blank unlined paper, rather than try to make lists.)

- No suggestions should be omitted.
- No suggestion should be discussed or criticized.

The point is to amass the maximum number of suggestions, and more ideas than you'll eventually need, but you won't decide which to keep until later.

■ The suggestions should not be sorted into groups. This is for later too.

Stage two of brainstorming is completely different. It is a one-person job which is evaluative, critical, focused and logical. It consists of:

■ going through all the ideas that have been collected;
■ scrubbing out the daft ones;
■ sorting the others into groups;
■ highlighting the best of them.

Activity 17  20 mins

Get together a group of colleagues (or your team) and try brainstorming the causes of Bill's problem – that is, the things that may have changed in January.

Jot down your ideas on a separate piece of paper. When you've finished, sort your ideas into groups.

Below is just one possible outcome of a brainstorming session on Bill's problem. The groups of causes selected are shown in the diagram (opposite). Your brainstorming session may well have come up with some different groups and lists of causes.

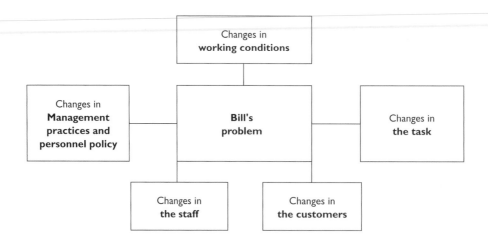

Brainstorming the possible causes of Bill's problem

All the suggestions have been grouped under the five headings, but the 'critical weeding' stage of the process has not yet begun.

Changes in the working conditions:

- relocation to smaller space;
- worse conditions;
- heating not adequate – hard to work;
- overcrowding;
- bad smells (ventilation problem);
- tools and equipment worn out, inadequate.

Changes in the task:

- increase in number of jobs to do;
- individual jobs harder to do;
- more processes, so longer to complete;
- new kinds of jobs – not so familiar;
- bigger proportion of faults – production problem;
- safety measures slowing down work.

Changes in the customers:

- getting more demanding;
- increased sales;
- different type of customers – don't know how to use product;
- change in distribution structure – more direct sales, so complaints coming back to us rather than to dealers?

Changes in the staff:

- experienced people have left – new ones not so quick;
- fall in morale for some other reason – Pay cuts? Fear of redundancy? Change of management? New working practices?
- Bill is new to the job – hasn't got leadership skills;
- jealousy over Bill's appointment.

Changes in management practice/personnel policy:

- boss not setting priorities properly;
- too much meddling;
- different priorities set;
- more paperwork to complete;
- safety measures slowing down work;
- Bill and/or team given additional tasks not mentioned?

Note that some causes, for example 'safety measures slowing down work', may appear in more than one group. On the other hand, some of the causes listed under some headings could be linked. Under 'Working conditions', 'relocation to smaller space' and 'overcrowding' are the same thing, while 'worse conditions' is a general term that could cover all of these.

6.3 Avoiding false assumptions

One of the commonest ways of taking the wrong path towards a solution is to make false assumptions. One of the benefits of brainstorming causes and solutions is that this is less likely to happen, because you are forced to consider all the options.

Activity 18

10 mins

Imagine you are concerned about the high turnover rate of staff in your department: too many are leaving and finding other jobs. You ask some of your staff what they think the problem is, and they suggest that a pay increase will help. As a result, you go to your boss and recommend a general pay increase.

What assumptions are you making? Why might some of these assumptions not be valid?

_____

_____

_____

After the exercise we have just carried out on Bill's problem, this should be clear to you. You are assuming:

■ that you have discovered the cause (or at least a major cause) of the staff turnover problem (but what about work conditions, environment, motivation, and so on?);

■ that increasing pay will reduce staff losses (but will it in the long term?);

■ that the increased wage bill will not help to make your organization's products unprofitable or uncompetitive, so threatening everyone's jobs.

You may have thought of other assumptions.

When you're trying to analyse a problem, always ask yourself what assumptions you are making. Are your assumptions valid? Questioning your assumptions will help you find the right cause and consequently the right solution.

Using a problem analysis technique will help you identify false assumptions and pinpoint the problem more accurately.

6.4 Probing for the truth

When you're trying to understand a problem, it's always useful to keep asking questions.

To illustrate this, let's return to Bill's problem.

> To quote Bill once again:
>
> 'The work just keeps piling up. I have to divide the team's time between repairing rejects sent over from Production and faulty items that are returned by customers. The boss is constantly telling me that this or that customer has complained about slow service, but he won't let us have any more staff. He just says I should get better organized. Production keep sending me more and more rejects, and they're always pressuring us too. Everyone's fed up, I'm fed up, and it's getting harder and harder to face it all.'

Asking 'why?' is something you will usually need to do in your own head, with a pencil and paper to help. You might perhaps imagine there are two voices speaking – one asking questions, and the other answering. Here's how it might go in Bill's case.

Why is the factory sending you more and more rejects?

Bill: I suppose they're increasing their output. I don't know for sure.

Is there another explanation? Is quality falling? Why don't you find out?

Bill: I could have a word with old Ted. Now I come to think of it, there's a rumour that they've been having trouble with parts suppliers. Perhaps Ted's in as much of a mess as I am.

Why is your boss so adamant about staffing levels?

Bill: Well, I agreed those staffing levels at the time of the budget, and he's a stickler for keeping to the figures. At budget time, though, we were running along smoothly.

Why are the two functions of factory repairs and customer repairs done within the same group?

Bill: A good question. In my last job we didn't do things that way. It means that I have to answer to two groups, effectively. Perhaps this is the crux of the problem. The system works well as long as we can cope with the workload. When we can't it means that I'm torn in two directions.

Would your boss listen to a well-presented argument for doing it differently?

And so on.

Activity 19 · 3 mins

What is the general outcome now? Do you think that after this mental discussion Bill would go back to his job in a more positive frame of mind?

_____

_____

There would be a very positive outcome from such an imaginary question-and-answer session. Now Bill has some ideas to think about, and he may be able to come up with some new approaches to his difficulties.

6.5 Fishbones: a way of analysing problems

Fishbone diagrams – also called cause-effect diagrams – are a simple visual technique for analysing problems where many possible causes may need to be considered. They can be drawn up from scratch, or built up from ideas developed by brainstorming.

The figure below is a fishbone diagram showing the five main groups of possible causes for 'Bill's problem'.

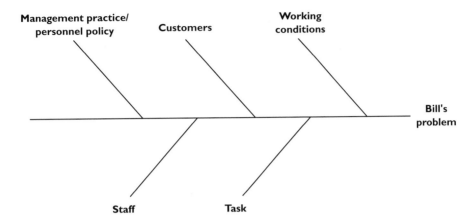

At the head of the fish is Bill's problem – unable to meet competing demands. Radiating from its spine are the five main groups of causes listed in the figure on page 26.

The next stage is to attach the more specific possible causes identified within each group (below).

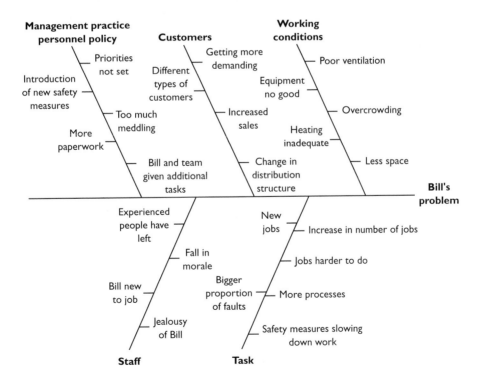

Once you have depicted all possible causes on a single sheet in this way, you can start to assess them individually.

The value of fishbone analysis is that:

- it gives you a **complete picture** of all the possibilities;
- it may enable you to discover that **more than one cause is involved**.

6.6 Drawing on experience

Experience – and learning – are of great help in problem solving. We often recognize, perhaps without even thinking about it, that a new problem is the same as, or similar to, one we've seen before.

Few problems are absolutely unique, and you will often find that you can apply general lessons that you've learned elsewhere.

Lakshmi supervises a group of machinists in a clothing factory. Every few days the manager calls her into the office and gives her the specifications for ranges of garments that have to be put into production by a certain date. It's then up to Lakshmi to organize her team to complete the jobs on time.

Lakshmi is an active member of her local school's Parent-Teacher Association, and one day, out of the blue, she is asked to help organize the annual fête. At first, Lakshmi is very nervous about it, as she hasn't done the job before. She starts to write down some headings.

- What sort of fête do the PTA members want?
- Where will the fête be held?
- When will it be held?
- Who is available to help me?
- What can they do?

Lakshmi soon realizes that organizing the fête isn't really so different from organizing her team to make a new line of garments.

Activity 20 · 3 mins

How many 'points of similarity' can you find between organizing the fête and the organizing that Lakshmi normally has to do at work?

_____

_____

_____

_____

_____

The tasks appear to be quite similar in a number of ways.

- A specification has to be agreed ('what sort of fête?').
- Activities have to be planned to meet deadlines.
- People have to be organized.
- Information has to be communicated.
- Tasks have to be allocated.

There are also, however, some clear differences. For one thing, when she is at work, Lakshmi has authority to get things done. She is also very familiar with all the activities and processes involved. The fête isn't like that: she'll have to lead and motivate people who have no strong obligation to be helpful.

Other people are also a storehouse of knowledge and experience, and it makes sense to draw on these. Even if you've never come across a particular problem before, one of your colleagues almost certainly has.

Bear in mind that simply talking with someone about a problem can do a lot to help you get it clear in your mind.

6.7 Using rules and procedures

Rules, procedures, guidelines, manuals and handbooks are all designed to make problem solving and decision making easier by **telling you what to do** in a range of situations. In fact, it's useful to think of them as concentrated experience in written form.

Computer buffs often say 'If all else fails, read the manual'.

It's amazing how often people ignore rules, instructions and guidelines, a[nd] get into difficulties as a result. You can probably think of instances of th[is] yourself.

Activity 21

5 mins

Here are five problems to which the answer might lie in a rulebook, manu[al,] set of guidelines, etc. Consider each problem from your own point of vie[w] and write down which documents might provide you with help in finding [a] solution.

1   A team member has breached safety regulations, and you are not sure wh[at] disciplinary action is appropriate.

_____

_____

2   You need to replace some equipment, but the supplier you favour is not know[n] to the organization. How can you establish whether the supplier is reliable?

_____

_____

3   Kelly wants to take some extra days of unpaid leave in addition to her annu[al] holiday. Can you sanction this?

_____

_____

4   Some valuables have gone missing from a team member's desk overnigh[t.] What should you do?

_____

_____

5   A customer has written a long letter complaining about a member of you[r] staff. How should you take this forward?

_____

_____

It's perfectly possible that some of these points are not covered by any rules, guidelines or handbooks in your particular organization. However, larger organizations will have all of them in writing somewhere. For example:

1 The health and safety handbook or the staff handbook will state what constitutes a disciplinary offence, and how it should be handled.

2 Where purchases can only be made from suppliers on an approved list, a procedure exists for suppliers to be added to it.

3 Rules about holiday entitlement, including how special requests are handled, will be in the staff handbook.

4 A security manual explains the procedure in cases of suspected theft.

5 This is perhaps the problem least likely to be covered by a written-down procedure. As a general rule such matters would be taken up by a suitably senior figure, possibly two levels above the person about whom the complaint was made.

There are also bound to be **people** who know the ins and outs of these policies and procedures.

Self-assessment 1

10 mins

1 Rearrange these words to complete the definition below:

The definition of a problem is: **deal difficult is or resolve something to which with.**

_____

2 Here are the six stages of problem solving. Fill in the blank spaces using either the word **problem** or the word **solution**.

Stage 1: **recognize** the _____

Stage 2: accept **ownership** of the _____

Stage 3: **understand** the _____

Stage 4: **choose** the best _____

Stage 5: **implement** the _____

Stage 6: monitor and **evaluate** the _____

3   Define the three main types of problem:

a deviation problems

_____

_____

b potential problems

_____

_____

c improvement problems

_____

_____

4   There is a simple test of whether you can define a problem clearly. What is it?

_____

5   One item is missing from this list of questions that appear on a problem statement. What is it?

Describe the problem briefly:

What effect is it having?

Where is it?

_____

Is there anything special or distinctive about it?

6   Here are three 'don'ts' to remember when brainstorming for causes or solutions. Fill in the blanks so that they make sense.

Don't omit any _____.

Don't _____ or _____ any suggestions.

Don't try to _____ the suggestions into _____.

7   What does a fishbone analysis give you?

_____

8   Complete the words below to explain why rules, procedures, manuals and handbooks can help you solve a problem:

Because they are:

c _____ e _____ in w _____ f _____.

Answers to these questions can be found on pages 125–6.

7 Summary

- It's a good idea to think about the problem before coming up with a solution.

- You are likely to encounter three main kinds of problem:
  - deviation problems, where something has gone wrong;
  - potential problems, ones that may be arising for the future;
  - improvement problems, where you try to find ways of improving performance.

- It is better to foresee and prevent problems than to wait till they have burst into the open. Most 'unforeseen' problems **could have been** anticipated.

- The six stages of problem solving that are described in this workbook are:
  - Stage 1: **recognize** the problem;
  - Stage 2: accept **ownership** of the problem;
  - Stage 3: **understand** the problem;
  - Stage 4: **choose** the best solution;
  - Stage 5: **implement** the solution;
  - Stage 6: monitor and **evaluate** the solution.

- You should not waste time and energy trying to solve problems that are:
  - likely to go away of their own accord;
  - unimportant;
  - best dealt with by someone else.

- It's worth asking yourself:
  - Is there a solution to this problem?
  - Will solving it be worth the effort?
  - What price am I prepared to pay for solving it?

- When you accept ownership of a problem you are making a promise that you must be sure to keep.

- When problems are difficult or complex, they need to be defined with care, preferably with the help of a **problem statement**.

- You may need to define the problem from more than one viewpoint.

- It's useful to identify **distinctive features** about a problem: these may give a strong clue to the cause(s).

- You will need to **collect information** to find the causes of problems and possible solutions.

- If possible, draw up a **problem analysis** showing what the problem is, and what it could be, but is not.

- **Brainstorming** is a valuable tool for helping to solve problems. There are two stages:
  - the first wide-ranging, uncritical and creative;
  - the second critical and focused.

- When thinking about a problem, try to avoid making **unwarranted assumptions**.

- Probe into the truth by continually asking questions.

- Use whatever **assistance** you can get to help you find the causes of a problem, including:
  - your own and other people's experience;
  - manuals, rules, procedures, guidelines, handbooks, etc.

Session B
Analysing information for solving problems and making decisions

1 Introduction

Most of this session (and some of the next) is about how you can analyse numerical information to inform the problem-solving and decision-making process. This includes analysing it in ways that will probably be very familiar such as totals and percentages and how you can use basic statistics to gain a better understanding of it.

You may have bad memories of statistics if you've ever done any before, but don't worry. Mostly we'll be suggesting that you use a spreadsheet to do the painful calculations – all you have to do is enter a few figures and understand what the results mean.

We'll also look at some of the **tools** available in **spreadsheets** that help you to sort, filter and analyse large amounts of data at the touch of a button.

Finally, we'll spend a short while thinking about how non-numerical data – generally words – can be analysed by imposing various structures on it and using cross-references and indexes.

1.1 Data and information

Facts and figures are called **data**.

Information is processed data.

Items of data do not usually convey any meaning on their own. Here is an example of data.

213   242   299   359   592

Activity 22

2 mins

What do these numbers and letters tell you?

_____

_____

_____

The best that most people could say is that there are five numbers rising by different amounts and ranging from 213 to 592. They could mean almost anything: the number of passengers on different trains; the weekly wages of five different employees. They could be dates (21 March, 24 February, February 1999, and so on).

Even if you happened to know what these numbers are they don't tell you anything on their own without further analysis.

Information is data that has been **analysed or processed** in some way so as to become **meaningful**, like this.

Country name	International dialling code
Algeria	213
Congo	242
Greenland	299
Bulgaria	359
Guyana	592

This data has simply been organized into a table with column headings and labels, but now you know exactly what it means.

Activity 23

How could the data be even better organized?

_____

_____

The answer to this Activity can be found on page 128.

 # 2 Analysing numerical data

EXTENSION 2
*Managing Information
and Statistics* by Roland
Bee and Frances Bee
is helpful for those
needing to know more
about this area of
management.

Organizations generate extensive amounts of numerical data, for example number of products sold, number of hours worked.

In most organizations this information is collected by the accounting system, and modern accounting software has highly sophisticated reporting capabilities. Analysing numerical data on a day-to-day basis may often simply be a case of knowing which buttons to press.

In this section, we are concerned with the less routine tasks of management. One example is analysing a collection of data that is not formally recorded by the accounting system, for example how long it takes to do a set of tasks in order to solve a problem.

Statistics is a word that frightens many people, and at an advanced level it can get very difficult. Most business statistics, however, involve simple techniques such as adding, subtracting, multiplying and dividing. And as you probably know, a spreadsheet can take almost all the effort out of handling numbers.

2.1 Ratios, indexes and percentages

It is often useful to measure one set of data against another to create a ratio or index.

For example, a business that occupies 128,000 m² of floor space and turns over £3,968,000 has a floor space to turnover ratio of 128:3,968. Last year the ratio was 125:3,375, while the average for businesses of this type was 1:36.

We can simplify these rather clumsy expressions by dividing the first number into the second (for instance 3,968/128 = 31). This gives us:

- this year's ratio (1:31);
- last year's ratio (1:27);
- the average for businesses of this type (1:36).

By reducing all the ratios to the same numerical base (i.e. 1), we make them easy to compare. This information shows us that the business is using its floor space more efficiently than last year, but not as efficiently as its competitors.

One of the best-known ratios is **profitability**, which is profit:capital employed (it is also known as return on capital employed, or ROCE).

Activity 24

4 mins

The table below shows the capital employed and annual profit of six different companies. Work out the profitability ratio and profit percentage and enter the figures in the blank columns. Calculate ratios to the nearest whole number and percentages to one decimal point. We have done the first calculation for you.

1   Profitability ratio = 995,400 / 15.80 = 1:63,000
    (This gives a ratio of profit per £ million capital employed.)

2   Profit percentage = (995,400 / 15,800,000) × 100% = 6.3%
    (This gives rate of profit per £100 capital employed.)

Company	Capital employed (£m)	2004 profit (£)	Capital:profit ratio	Profit %
A	15.80	995,400	1:63,000	6.3
B	5.90	324,500	1:	
C	44.20	5,348,200	1:	
D	21.40	2,461,000	1:	
E	0.85	79,000	1:	
F	87.00	13,746,000	1:	

Most profitable: _____

Least profitable: _____

The answer to this Activity can be found on page 129.

You will probably realize, having done this Activity, that percentages are often easier to understand than ratios, though the calculation is much the same.

Ratios and percentages are both ways of presenting relationships so as to make it easier to compare figures. Here is another example.

	2003				2004	
	Qtr 1	Qtr 2	Qtr 3	Qtr 4	Qtr 1	Qtr 2
Revenue (£000s)	1,630	1,752	1,871	2,558	1,595	1,804
Headcount	49	47	44	57	40	40

Look across the table rows and see how both sets of figures are going up and down. We can probably assume that this is a seasonal business which performs strongly in the period up to Christmas and experiences a sharp fall afterwards. Extra staff members are taken on for the Christmas quarter.

On their own, these figures tell us nothing about the efficiency of this business. However, if we create a ratio of **revenue per headcount** (in other words divide revenue by headcount), the picture becomes much clearer.

Ratio of revenue to headcount

	2003				2004	
	Qtr 1	**Qtr 2**	**Qtr 3**	**Qtr 4**	**Qtr 1**	**Qtr 2**
	£000	£000	£000	£000	£000	£000
£000 per head	33.27	37.28	42.52	44.88	39.88	45.10

Later in this session we'll see how we might predict Quarter 4 sales in 2004, when we look at forecasting and moving averages.

Productivity is another good example of the value of ratios. We calculate it as a measure of output against a measure of labour. Output is usually measured in units, while labour may be measured in various ways, such as:

- payroll headcount;
- payroll cost;
- hours worked;
- cost per head.

These four ratios may produce somewhat different results, as the next Activity will show.

Activity 25

Period	1	2	3	4	5	Average
Data						
Output (units)	217.0	221.0	229.0	214.0	233.0	
Headcount	61.0	61.0	59.0	51.0	51.0	
Cost (£'000s)	119.6	125.3	125.1	119.5	131.3	
Hours worked	2,318.0	2,379.0	2,315.0	2,116.0	2167.0	
Indexes						
Output per head						
Cost per unit of output						
Hours worked per unit						
Cost per head						

Work out the productivity indexes and averages, and insert them in the blank spaces in the table. Show your answers to two decimal places.

What do the indexes and averages show?

_____

_____

_____

_____

_____

The correct version of the table, and our interpretation, can be found on page 129.

Note that measuring, recording and producing indexes from this data – that is, **analysing** it – has resulted in:

- a clear picture of how the productivity position has been changing;
- recognition that there is a problem;
- a clear identification of where the problem lies.

2.2 What is 'typical'?

Managers can learn a lot from figures using the simplest of techniques: counting, adding, dividing, and calculating percentages and indexes.

Usually this involves putting data into some kind of table and working out totals and averages. (We'll talk in general about how to lay out tables in Session C: you have already seen lots of examples in this session and the last.)

Let's take, as a very basic example, interviews conducted by three staff at a government office. The staff members work a five-day, 37.5 hour week.

Activity 26 · 4 mins

We start by counting how many interviews each person carried out each day.

Work out the totals and enter them in the blank column of the table below. (The average (or 'mean') is the total divided by the number of working days. Do the average to one decimal place.)

These calculations can easily be done by hand using a calculator, but if you have access to a spreadsheet, this is a better option. For example, if you start entering data at cell A1 you could use the formulae =SUM(B2:F2) and =AVERAGE(B2:F2).

Staff	Interviews conducted per day						
	Monday	Tuesday	Wednesday	Thursday	Friday	Total	Average
Dela	45	43	44	21	46		
Corinne	54	50	51	55	53		
David	38	41	40	44	39		

The answer to this Activity can be found on page 130.

Next we add some extra data for comparison purposes, showing target performance – the number of interviews each person is expected to carry out.

We can now do some more complex and informative calculations:

- the percentage of target performance achieved (actual performance divided by target performance × 100%);
- the average performance.

Activity 27

6 mins

Work out these percentages and averages and enter them in this table to show performance against target. Work to one decimal place. Use a spreadsheet and SUM and AVERAGE formulae if possible.

Staff	Interviews conducted per day						
	Monday	**Tuesday**	**Wednesday**	**Thursday**	**Friday**	**Total**	**Average**
Dela							
Actual	45.0	43.0	44.0	21.0	46.0		
Target	52.5	52.5	52.5	52.5	52.5		
% of target						n/a	
Corinne							
Actual	54.0	50.0	51.0	55.0	53.0		
Target	52.5	52.5	52.5	52.5	52.5		
% of target						n/a	
David							
Actual	38.0	41.0	40.0	44.0	39.0		
Target	38.0	38.0	38.0	38.0	38.0		
% of target						n/a	

The answer to this Activity can be found on page 130.

By processing the data in these quite simple ways, we can obtain some use[ful] information from them.

- How each person is performing against target.
- How each person is performing against the departmental average.

The new figures also reveal some unexplained oddities.

Activity 28 · 2 mins

Note down two things that strike you as odd about the final figures.

_____

_____

There are two obvious points.

- On Thursday, Dela's performance fell sharply to 21 interviews.
- David's target figures are lower than those for the other two staff.

Managers are always looking for deviations from what is expected, so thes[e] two oddities need to be explained. An investigation may discover, fo[r] instance, that Dela was sick for an afternoon, and that David is a trainee wh[o] has been set lower targets initially. Or perhaps Dela spent an afternoon si[t]ting with David, helping with training.

Whatever the case you should investigate the cause of the variation. Analys[is] of data can identify where problems may be occurring or how frequently the[y] then occur. It doesn't tell you why.

2.3 Measures of central tendency

You hear about averages all the time — average income, average lifespan, aver[age] number of goals per game or runs per innings, and so on.

Averages like this can be useful because they can often answer the questio[n] 'what is typical?'.

The most common type of average is more properly called the **arithmetic mean**, and it is very easy to calculate: you simply find the total of the numbers, then divide by the number of values. If you have three values, 1, 2 and 3, the total is 6 and so the arithmetic mean is 6 divided by 3, which equals 2: (1 + 2 + 3) / 3 = 2.

However, an average like this can be 'mean' in the sense that it doesn't tell you all you need to know: it can be misleading. The performance figures we just looked at for Dela are a case in point. It is important for her manager to know her typical performance against target, but averaging her across five days does not give an accurate idea of what is typical.

Because Dela only worked for half the day on Thursday, her average performance over five days comes out as 75.8%. If we'd omitted Thursday, her average would be 84.8%, and this is a truer reflection of her performance.

The mean can easily be distorted by the inclusion of one or more untypical figures, so it sometimes helps to use a different measure of centrality.

Two alternatives to the mean are the **median** and the **mode.**

- The **median** is the **middle value** in a series.
- The mode is the value which appears **most often** in a series.

Activity 29

| 179 | 199 | 202 | 229 | 249 | 263 | 263 | 263 | 277 |

In the nine-value series above, determine the average (arithmetic mean), the median and the mode.

_____

_____

_____

What formulae would you use to determine the arithmetic mean (average), the median, and the mode if these figures were entered in cells A1 to A9 of a spreadsheet? (This question is much easier than you might think!)

_____

_____

_____

The answers to this Activity can be found on page 131.

There is sometimes a case for saying that either the median or the mode pr⟨o⟩vides a more meaningful answer to the question 'what is typical?' than t⟨he⟩ mean does.

2.4 Grouped data

Suppose you measure the daily demand for a product you are selling ov⟨er⟩ 20 days and then want to analyse the results to find typical daily dema⟨nd⟩. For instance, in the following results there were two days when daily dema⟨nd⟩ was 14.

Daily demand	Frequency
14	2
22	2
24	1
27	1
30	3
31	6
32	2
33	1
39	1
50	1

How can you calculate the average?

One way, of course, is not to group the data like this in the first place. Y⟨ou⟩ could simply list out a value for each of the 20 days and divide the sum by 2⟨0⟩.

A quicker way, however – and sometimes the only way, depending on t⟨he⟩ data – is to multiply daily demand by frequency and then divide by 20.

Daily demand (x)	Frequency (f)	Daily demand time⟨s⟩ frequency (fx)
14	2	28
22	2	44
24	1	24
27	1	27
30	3	90
31	6	186
32	2	64
33	1	33
39	1	39
50	1	50
	20	585

The average is 585/20 = 29.25.

This technique becomes especially useful if you are asked to work out an average from data that is collected in **class** intervals. For instance, using the previous example data might have been shown as follows.

Daily demand	Frequency
1 to 10	0
11 to 20	2
21 to 30	7
31 to 40	10
41 to 50	1
	20

This makes it more difficult to find the average because a certain amount of detail has been lost. To calculate the average when we have grouped data like this we need to decide which value best represents all of the values in a particular class interval.

It is a convention in statistics to take the mid-point of each class interval, on the assumption that the frequencies occur pretty evenly.

Daily demand	Mid-point x	Frequency f	fx
1 to 10	5	0	0
11 to 20	15	2	30
21 to 30	25	7	175
31 to 40	35	10	350
41 to 50	45	1	45
		20	600

Arithmetic mean = 600/20 = 30.

Because our assumption that frequencies occur evenly within each class interval was not quite correct, this answer is not exactly right, but it is pretty close to the actual average of 29.25 (and we probably can't sell 0.25 of a product anyway).

In fact, although we won't demonstrate it, as the frequencies get larger (for instance, if you measured a year's worth of daily sales), the size of this error would steadily get smaller.

There is another example. In a particular week, the wages earned by 69 employees were as follows.

Wages	Number of employees
Up to £150	4
£151 to £160	10
£161 to £170	12
£171 to £180	13
£181 to £190	16
£191 to £200	8
£201 or more	6
	69

We don't know the mid-point of the range 'under £150' but since all other class intervals are £10 we assume it is £145. Likewise we assume the mid-point of the range '£201 or more' is £205.

Mid-point £	Frequency	Mid-point × Frequency
145	4	580
155	10	1,550
165	12	1,980
175	13	2,275
185	16	2,960
195	8	1,560
205	6	1,230
	69	12,135

The arithmetic mean is 12,135/69 = £175.87.

2.5 The range

Unfortunately there are situations where focusing on one typical or central number, such as the mean, median or mode, still doesn't really help us understand what is going on.

In such a case we need to look at the **spread** of the data.

Measures of spread (or dispersion) give you some idea of how widely the data you have is spread about its average.

The **range**, for instance, is simply the difference between the highest value and the lowest value.

Activity 30

Calculate the mean and the range of each of the following sets of data. (The range can be calculated on a spreadsheet using a formula such as =MAX(A1:A8)–MIN(A1:A8).)

1   4, 8, 7, 3, 5, 16, 24, 5
2   10, 7, 9, 11, 11, 8, 9, 7

What do your calculations show about the spread of the data?

_____

_____

_____

_____

1   The first set of eight figures add up to 72, so they have a mean of 9. The range is 24 (highest value) – 3 (lowest value) = 21.

2   The second set of eight figures add up to 72, so they also have a mean of 9. However, the range is 11 – 7 = 4.

The first set of data is more widely dispersed than the second set. The lower the range, the less widely spread the data is.

2.6 Quartiles

Quartiles are a commonly-used way of identifying the range within which the values in a set of data occur. Quartiles often are used in sales and marketing research, and in education. Whereas the median is the value half way through a set of data, quartiles are the values one-quarter and three-quarters of the way through. The median divides the data in half; quartiles find the midpoint of each half.

Suppose you have a set of values in cells B2 to B2357 in an Excel spreadsheet and you want to find the median, lower quartile and upper quartile.

You can do this using formulae.

=QUARTILE(B2:B2357,1) will give you the lower quartile.
=QUARTILE(B2:B2357,2) will give you the median.
=QUARTILE(B2:B2357,3) will give you the upper quartile.

For the median you can also use =MEDIAN (B2:B2357,2).

Note that this will not work in all spreadsheet packages and you will need to consult your package's 'Help' facility if you are using another package.

Activity 31

Here is a set of sales results for a week in December and a week in June for 15 sales staff. The product is a seasonal one, which sells much better in the summer. Identify the lower and upper quartiles and the median for each sitting and suggest how these figures might be used.

December 2003	June 2004
4	39
14	40
16	48
18	54
20	55
22	67
23	69
25	73
26	78
29	78
31	78
33	80
39	81
42	94
47	97

Identify the lower and upper quartiles and the median for each period and suggest how these figures might be used.

_____

_____

_____

_____

_____

Using a spreadsheet we find the following values.

	December 2003	June 2004
Lower quartile	19	54.5
Median	25	73
Upper quartile	32	79

This information could prove useful in planning sales targets.

In December 2004 you might set the target at the median figure of 25 units.

In June 2005, however, anyone who was selling at a rate of about 25 units in December might be expected to sell around 73 units.

Any of the sales staff who sold fewer than 55 in June would be falling seriously below target, while anyone who achieved sales of more than 79 units might be eligible for a high sales for the month award. Similar figures could be calculated for December rates of sales.

2.7 The inter-quartile range

The lower and upper quartiles can be used to calculate a measure of dispersion called the inter-quartile range. The inter-quartile range is the difference between the values of the upper and lower quartiles and hence shows the range of values of the **middle half** of the set of data. The smaller the inter-quartile range, the less dispersed the data. Because values at the ends are not taken into account, the inter-quartile range is not affected by extreme values.

For example, if the lower and upper quartiles of a set of numbers were 6 and 11, the inter-quartile range would be $11 - 6 = 5$. This shows that the range of values of the middle half of the population is 5 units.

2.8 The standard deviation

EXTENSION 3
For more help with statistics, Lloyd Jaisingh's *Statistics for the Utterly Confused* is a good guide.

Because it only uses the middle 50% of the data, the inter-quartile range can be a useful measure of spread if there are extreme values.

However, it may often seem unreasonable to exclude 50% of the data.

The standard deviation (SD) is a measure of the amount by which the values in a set of numbers differ from the arithmetic mean. It is calculated using **all** of the data, not just half of it. You can calculate the SD manually or using a scientific calculator, but the easiest way is to use a spreadsheet.

Activity 32

Most of the following numbers are in the range 50 to 75, but there are some extreme values at either end.

Enter the numbers into cells A1 to A10 of a spreadsheet and find the standard deviation using the formula =STDEVP(A1:A10). Work to two decimal places.

5	20	52	60	62	64	72	72	82	151

You should get the answer 36.88 (rounded).

Although this might not look like a very meaningful number the standard deviation is actually an incredibly useful statistic because it can be proved that:

- **68%** of the values in a set of numbers will fall within **one standard deviation** of the arithmetic mean;
- **95%** of the values in a set of numbers will fall within **two standard deviations** of the mean.

Once you know this, the SD can be used in a wide variety of business situations, simply by collecting a relatively small sample of data: for example, in quality control, to predict future performance and prepare budgets. (We won't go into the theory, which is quite complex.)

In this case the arithmetic mean is 64. The only value that is beyond 2 standard deviations is the very extreme value 151.

−2SD	−1SD	Mean	+1SD	+2SD
−9.76	27.12	64	100.88	137.76

2.9 Forecasting and moving averages

Finally, in this 'statistics' part of the session, we'll take a look at another use of averages to help manage a business – averages to help with anticipating the future.

One of the most important forecasts an organization has to make is the sales forecast. How can an organization estimate how much it is likely to sell?

There are several mathematical techniques for sales forecasting such as regression analysis and exponential smoothing, which are a bit too complex for this book. Here we will concentrate on **moving averages** and **time series analysis**. The idea behind calculating a moving average is to eliminate seasonal variations.

Suppose that sales of a product for the past four years have been as follows.

Year	Season	Sales (£)
2000	Spring	5,100
	Summer	2,900
	Autumn	7,600
	Winter	4,600
2001	Spring	5,300
	Summer	3,600
	Autumn	7,500
	Winter	4,300
2002	Spring	4,900
	Summer	3,900
	Autumn	7,800
	Winter	5,200
2003	Spring	5,400
	Summer	3,800
	Autumn	8,500
	Winter	4,900

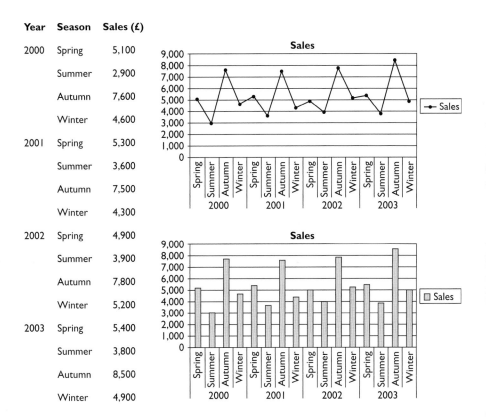

A clear pattern can be seen, especially if you look at the graph or the bar chart. But how can this organization forecast sales for 2004?

Using the moving averages technique, you begin by establishing what the seasonal cycle is. Here it is the four seasons of the year and a one year cycle. (In another situation, it might be a weekly cycle of seven days.)

Next, you calculate the **moving average** of 12-monthly sales, and from this, the moving average of seasonal sales. The idea behind calculating a moving average is to eliminate seasonal variations.

Moving averages are matched against the **mid-point** of the time period to which they relate. The figures in the table are explained below it.

			Four season total	Centred average	Seasonal average (Trend)	Variation
2000	Spring	5,100				
	Summer	2,900				
			20,200			
	Autumn	7,600		20,300	5075.0	2525.0
			20,400			
	Winter	4,600				
			Etc.			
2001	Spring	5,300				

- **Four season total**: the first figure is the sum of the sales for Spring to Winter 2000 (5,100 + 2,900 + 7,600 + 4,600 = 20,200); the second is the sum of sales for Summer 2000 to Spring 2001 (2,900 + 7,600 + 4,600 + 5,300 = 20,400), and so on.

- **Centred average**: a new average is then obtained and lined up directly with the appropriate time period by taking a further average of each pair of total 12-monthly sales, for instance the average of the first two totals 20,200 and 20,400 is 20,300.

- **Seasonal average or trend**: this is simply the centred average divided by the number of seasons: 20,300/4 = 5,075. This shows the underlying long-term movement in the values. In this example we can now see clearly that there is an underlying upward trend in sales.

- **Variation**: this is the difference between the seasonal average and the actual sales: 7,600 − 5,075 = 2,525.

However, to make the data easy to set up on a spreadsheet, it is better to set it out as shown below.

		Four season total	Centred average	Seasonal average (Trend)	Variation
2000	Spring	5,100			
	Summer	2,900			
	Autumn	7,600		20,300	5075.0	2,525.0
	Winter	4,600	20,200	20,750	5187.5	−587.5
2001	Spring	5,300	20,400	21,050	5262.5	37.5
	Summer	3,600	21,100	20,850	5212.5	−1,612.5
	Autumn	7,500	21,000	20,500	5125.0	2,375.0
	Winter	4,300	20,700	20,450	5112.5	−812.5
2002	Spring	4,900	20,300	20,750	5187.5	−287.5
	Summer	3,900	20,600	21,350	5337.5	−1,437.5
	Autumn	7,800	20,900	22,050	5512.5	2,287.5
	Winter	5,200	21,800	22,250	5562.5	−362.5
2003	Spring	5,400	22,300	22,550	5637.5	−237.5
	Summer	3,800	22,200	22,750	5687.5	−1,887.5
	Autumn	8,500	22,900			
	Winter	4,900	22,600			

The difference between the actual sales in each period and the trend is the **seasonal variation** in actual sales from the average seasonal sales. To obtain a best estimate of the future variation in sales each season, we now take the simple average of these figures, as follows (figures in round brackets are negative numbers).

	Spring	Summer	Autumn	Winter
Variation				
2000			2,525.0	(587.5)
2001	37.5	(1,612.5)	2,375.0	(812.5)
2002	(287.5)	(1,437.5)	2,287.5	(362.5)
2003	(237.5)	(1,887.5)		
Total	(487.5)	(4,937.5)	7,187.5	(1,762.5)
Average (divide by 3)	(162.5)	(1,645.8)	2,395.8	(587.5)

This gives us our estimated seasonal variations in sales for each season, above or below the average seasonal sales.

If we now estimate the total sales for 2004 to be, say 23,000 units, our detailed sales forecast for 2004 would be as follows.

	Average per quarter Units	Seasonal variation Units	Sales forecast Units
Spring	5,750	(162.5)	5,587.5
Summer	5,750	(1,645.8)	4,104.2
Autumn	5,750	2,395.8	8,145.8
Winter	5,750	(587.5)	5,162.5
	23,000	0.0	23,000.0

Activity 33 · 30 mins

1 Enter the original three columns of data for sales between 2000 and 2003 on a spreadsheet in cells A2 to C17. Then enter formulae to calculate the remaining figures shown above. You will have to give some further thought to layout to do this effectively.

2 Using your spreadsheet estimate the sales pattern for 2004 on the basis that the organization expects annual sales to be around 28,000 units.

The answer to this Activity can be found on page 131.

3 Non-numerical information

In the context of *Solving Problems and Decision Making* the term **qualitative information** is used to mean any information that is not numerical, but describes or explains things.

3.1 Structure

How can you organize such information? There are several ways, and you could use them alone or in combination.

- **By name**. In other words, in alphabetical order.

- **By date**. A date is a sort of number, of course, and information such as correspondence is most usefully organized in strict date order. Dates are also used in a less precise sense, however. For instance, you may organize a list of tasks to be done into those that have to be done by the end of this week, those that must be complete by next Wednesday, and so on.

- **By category**. This could be anything that items of information have in common with each other, for instance physical items may have a size or colour, staff could be categorized according to department or job title, and so on.

- **In logical sequence**. Many activities have to be done in a particular order. For instance, if you are making a cup of tea you put water in the kettle and then boil it before pouring it into the cup. That's an obvious example: with more complex work activities it is not always obvious what the most efficient sequence is.

- **In order of importance**. The most important items of information should be put first: typically these are things that will cost a lot of money, or take up a lot of time, or have a major impact on others.

Activity 34

Here is some information about some of the members of a customer services work team as at 3 March 2004.

Employee No.	Last name	First name	Position	Date joined	2004 Annual Review
CS0011	Saleem	Khalid	Manager	28/05/1997	28 May
CS0014	Howard	Corinne	Trainee	07/02/2003	Overdue
CS0035	Scott	Carla	Sales assistant	18/04/2002	18 April
CS0073	Bhat	Chandra	Sales assistant	11/02/1999	Overdue
CS0081	Smith	David	Sales assistant	10/10/2002	10 October
CS0094	Otsuka	Dave	Supervisor	08/06/1998	8 June

How is this information organized?

_____

How else might it be organized?

_____

_____

_____

How do you think it should be organized?

_____

_____

_____

The answer to this Activity can be found on page 131.

3.2 Report structure

Not all information can be presented in a list. This book, for instance, is full of information organized into sessions, which in turn are divided into sections, sub-sections, paragraphs, bullet points and activities.

You probably won't be asked to write a book in your job, but you will often have to write some kind of short report on operational matters for your managers to read. You may have to create or update some kind of procedures manual for your own team.

Various techniques can be used to make the content of such a document easy to identify and digest.

- The material in the report should be in a logical order.
- The relative importance of points should be signalled by headings.
- Each point may be numbered in some way to help with cross-reference.
- The document should be easy on the eye, helped by different font sizes, bold, italics, capitals, spacing, and so on.

A typical report structure has the following features.

- **Headings**. There is a hierarchy of headings. There is an overall title and the report as a whole is divided into sections. Within each section main points have a heading in bold capitals, sub-points have a heading in bold, lower-case and sub-sub-points have a heading in italics. (Three levels of headings within a main section is usually considered the maximum number that readers can cope with.) It is better not to underline headings. Underlining makes the page look 'busy' and gets in the way of the content.

- **References**. Sections are lettered A, B, and so on. Main points are numbered 1, 2, and so on, and within each division paragraphs are numbered 1.1, 1.2, 2.1, 2.2. Sub-paragraphs inherit their references from the paragraph above. For instance, the first sub-paragraph under paragraph 1.2 is numbered 1.2.1.
- **Fonts**. Word processors offer you a wealth of fonts these days, but it is best to avoid the temptation. It is often a good idea to put headings in a different font to the main text, but stop there: two fonts is quite enough.

Our example is not the only way of organizing a report, of course. You might choose to reference sub-paragraphs 1.2(a), 1.2(b), and so on. You might use roman numerals, although we advise against this. If your report turns out to be longer than you expected and you get up to paragraph XLVIII you are likely to confuse many of your readers unless they happen to be Romans.

The longer the document the better structured it needs to be. Large-scale reports or manuals may run to hundreds of pages, and will therefore require the following.

1　Title page
2　Contents list
3　Objective/term of reference
4　Summary
5　Introduction
6　Main body of the report
7　Conclusions
8　Recommendations
9　Appendices

Appendices are commonly used for:

- background information that will not be required by all readers;
- statistical information, which has been abstracted or interpreted in the body of the report;
- documents referred to in the report.

Activity 35

Some organizations have what is known as a 'house style' for documents, reports, presentations and similar documents. This is a set of rules that specifies details such as hierarchies of headings, paragraph numbering system, spacing between paragraphs, fonts to use, size and placement of company logo, acceptable colours, and so on.

Develop a 'house style' for your own work team. The best way to do this is
find an existing document that is five to ten pages long and define a style f
each element.

Once you've worked out all the styles you may like to go further and create
word processing template for use in your department. Be sure to save a co

3.3 Cross-references

Cross-references are pointers to other places in the same document
to other information sources where related information can be found. Fe
instance, if paragraph 3.5 refers to a topic described in more detail later in tl
document you can save space and avoid repetition by saying 'See paragraph 6.

Activity 36 · 2 mins

Why is it better to cross-refer to a paragraph number than to a page numbe

The answer to this Activity can be found on page 131.

However, ultimately everything is related to everything else and if you are no
careful there could be no end to the cross-references. The best advice is t
keep them to a minimum, otherwise your readers will be forever flicking fro
one page to another, and will most likely lose the plot. If too many cros
references seem to be necessary it is probably time to consider re-arrangir
the information in your report.

3.4 Indexing

An index is an alphabetical list of the names, places and subjects dealt with in
document or book, giving the page or pages on which each item is mentione

Shorter documents should not usually need an index if there is good use c
headings and a reasonably detailed contents page. If you start to feel that you
document will be hard to follow without an index, it may be time to thin
about re-arranging the material into a more logical structure.

Longer documents – for instance a procedures manual – may well be improved by an index, so let's think about some of the issues.

Your first thought might be to do it by computer. Computers are both a help and a hindrance for indexing. It would be very quick and easy to compile an index listing every occurrence of every word in this session using a word processor. (Such a list is sometimes called a 'concordance'.) But the list would include a massive amount of irrelevant information: words like 'the', 'a', 'it', and so on, which no one would need to look up.

If you need to prepare an index you need to exercise some discretion. Suppose we wanted to index the occurrences of the word 'spreadsheet' in this session. You can easily do this with a word processor (for example Microsoft Word) by selecting one example of the word and choosing **Insert . . . Index . . . Mark Entry . . . Mark All.**

The result would be something like this (note: these are not the actual page numbers, this is just an example).

Spreadsheet 34, 37, 39, 44, 45, 46, 48, 49, 50, 51, 52, 53, 54, 55, 63

Activity 37 · 3 mins

How useful is a list like this to a reader?

_____

_____

Can you suggest how the list might be improved?

_____

_____

_____

It is not very useful at all because most of the references are just examples of where the word 'spreadsheet' is used in passing (for instance in Activities that say something like 'you might find it easier to do this with a spreadsheet'). And it would be very annoying for the reader to have to turn backwards and forwards through a document or book looking at each of 15 instances.

The list would be much improved if it organized the information according sub-topics that the reader might want to look up, like this.

Spreadsheet
data analysis with, 49
MEDIAN formula, 39, 96
QUARTILE formula, 44, 97

Note that the phrases in our example don't actually appear in the body of th session, so they can't simply be 'tagged' by a word processor.

A good index would also have separate entries under the appropriate lett and topic, for instance as follows.

Data analysis
with spreadsheet, 49

So, although indexing involves a little manipulating of words appearing in document or set of documents (which computers can do), it involves a l more of understanding and organizing the ideas and information in the doc ments, and anticipating the needs of users (which computers cannot do).

We have interrupted the six stage problem-solving process with this sessio to explore some of the ways that you can analyse both quantitative (nume ical) and qualitative (text) to inform the problem-solving and decision-maki process. Analysis of data can help to make the nature and scale of problen clearer, and can even show if the problem exists at all. If you practice th techniques you have learnt here you will find that you can understand pro lems more clearly and will make much better informed decisions.

Self-assessment 2

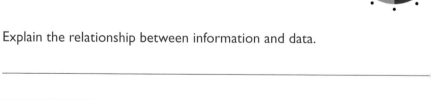

10 mins

1 Explain the relationship between information and data.

_____

_____

_____

2 Express these profit and capital figures as ratios with a numerical base of We have worked out the first one for you. It shows that Business A made £ profit for every £4.73 of capital.

Business	A	B	C	D
Profit	£128,000	£16,250	£3.57 million	£377,500
Capital	£605,000	£16,000	£11.5 million	£9 million
Ratio	1:4.73			

Which business is the most profitable?

_____

3   Here is a series of figures.

4.9   5.1   5.1   5.1   5.3   5.4   5.7   5.9   6.3   6.8   6.8

Find the mean, the median and the mode.

_____

_____

_____

4   ■ The upper quartile is the number that 75% of the values in a set of data are
    _____ or equal to.

What are the missing words: 'more than' or 'less than'?

    ■ The range only uses the middle half of the set of numbers.   True/False?

5   When are Pivot Tables useful?

_____

_____

6   Name five ways of organizing descriptive information.

_____

7   Besides a good word processor what two other things do you need to pre-
    pare a good index?

_____

_____

Answers to these questions can be found on page 126.

4 Summary

- Information is data that has been analysed or processed in some way so as to become meaningful.

- Most business statistics involve simple techniques such as adding, subtracting, multiplying and dividing. For instance, ratios and percentages are both very simple ways of presenting relationships so as to make it easier to compare figures.

- Averages give you an idea of what is typical. The most common type of average is called the arithmetic mean: the total of the numbers divided by the number of values. However, this can sometimes be misleading and two alternatives are the median (the middle value) and the mode (the value that appears most often).

- Grouped data summarizes more detailed figures, for instance you might say that five of the values fall in the range 0 to 10. To perform calculations with such data it is conventional to take the mid-point of each 'class interval', on the assumption that the frequencies occur pretty evenly.

- The spread of data can be measured by looking at the range or percentiles. A percentile is a number that a certain percentage of the values are less than or equal to. However, the most useful figure for statistical analysis is the standard deviation, which is a measure of the amount by which the values in a set of numbers differ from the arithmetic mean.

- Spreadsheets contain a number of tools that help to analyse lists of numerical and/or textual information. Sorting and filtering can be done at the touch of a button. Very complex analysis is possible with a PivotTable.

- Non-numerical lists of information may be organized alphabetically, chronologically, according to some common characteristic, in order of importance, and so on. Longer documents will need to be structured with headings, paragraph numbers and the like.

- Cross-references can save time and avoid repetition but should be kept to a minimum to avoid confusing the reader. Indexes can be useful in longer documents, but the indexer needs to understand the information very well and be able to anticipate the needs of users.

Session C
Finding a solution

▪ 1 Introduction

Very experienced people can often see a solution to a problem almost instantly; very **inexperienced** people also tend to go for 'instant solutions', though these often turn out to be the wrong ones. It is important to bear in mind that, until you are very experienced, it can pay to **delay** selecting a solution until you have thoroughly understood the problem.

In Session A we looked at the problem itself – what exactly is it? It is extremely easy to misunderstand problems, or to express them too vaguely, or to see them from only one point of view. We then went on to think about causes and considered some techniques for identifying what they might be. In Session B we looked at some of the techniques you can use to analyse problems to help you identify causes. In this session we have to match solutions to causes – which is not always as easy as it might seem. This is all about Stage 4 in the problem-solving process: **choosing a solution.**

▪ 2 Stage 4: choose a solution

Before we go on to this, here is some information you have perhaps been curious about – the cause of Bill's problem in Session A. In fact, analysis of the causes came to the following conclusions.

- Working conditions had not changed significantly, and were not considered to be a cause.
- **The task had changed**: introduction of a new product range had led to quality problems, with an increased proportion of 'bugs' being discovered.
- The customers had changed, in that they were becoming more demanding, but this was considered to be a general change in the market about which nothing could be done.
- The people (Bill and the team) had not changed significantly, so the cause did not lie in this area.
- **Management practices had changed**: under the pressure of customer complaints and production problems, Bill's line manager was intervening too much and failing to set clear priorities.

3 What is a solution?

This may seem a strange question: a solution is whatever solves the problem, you may say.

Actually, this is unrealistic, as the following three examples illustrate.

3.1 When a solution is not a solution

Gerry and Kate hadn't bought a TV licence. Two reminders came, which they ignored. One day they saw a detector van down the street. Problem! They ran upstairs and pretended no-one was in. They ignored the loud knock on the door. Two hours later they saw the detector van drive away.

Activity 38

1 min

Was their problem solved? Explain your answer.

_____

_____

_____

_____

Super-Utility Management plc ran a 'one-stop shop' inquiry service and helpline for their two million customers. Over a hundred operators worked shifts in rather crowded premises in the city centre. Capacity was limited, and there were increasing delays in answering calls. Since call response times were a 'key performance indicator' for the industry, there was clearly a problem. Management decided that in order to expand and improve the service, they would have to relocate.

They chose new premises at a green-field site about ten miles from the city centre. There was plenty of space for expansion, but the relocation proved to be a fiasco from the staff's point of view. There were no local facilities such as shops and banks, so they had to make extra trips when they needed these things. Second, the in-house facilities that they had been promised (a rest room and a proper canteen) were cut back to save costs: there was just a corridor to sit in and a couple of vending machines. Finally, and worst, many staff found the site difficult to get to. Almost everyone could get to and from the old city centre site by public transport, even late at night. Now only about a fifth of them could use public transport. Others had to rely on taxis, and several were forced to buy cars for the first time.

There was a sharp fall in morale, and recruitment became difficult. Performance, instead of rising, fell.

Activity 39 · 1 min

Was the relocation a solution to the problem? Explain your answer.

_____

_____

_____

_____

Paula and James decided that the new management trainee Serena was indeed an arrogant individual who would never fit in. They agreed that she would have to go. Paula didn't want to be seen to have picked 'a wrong 'un', so she and Bob decided to make Serena's life so difficult that she would resign.

Activity 40 · 1 min

Was this a solution to the problem? Explain your answer.

_____

_____

_____

_____

All three of these case studies featured 'solutions' that were not really solutions at all, though for different reasons.

- In the first case, hiding until the detector van has gone does not solve the problem. Sooner or later the detector van will return, and next time Greg and Kate may not be so lucky.

Postponing a problem doesn't solve it – though it may give you time to work out a solution.

■ In the second case, the company's 'solution' to deteriorating performance only succeeded in making the problem worse.

A bad solution can make old problems worse and create unexpected new ones.

■ In the last case, a solution that might well work should be rejected on moral, legal or policy grounds. Paula's proposal – essentially to drive Serena out of the company by treating her unfairly – would certainly be over-ruled by senior management. Note that Paula's reasons for selecting this option were dubious in themselves – she didn't want to have to sack Serena because this might reflect badly on her.

Some solutions are unacceptable.

3.2 Constraints on a solution

Solutions to problems are always subject to constraints – limitations on what you can do. For example, as we have just seen, there may be **moral, legal** and **policy** constraints on what solutions can be adopted.

Activity 41

5 mins

Think carefully about this question. What other constraints might affect your choice of a solution to any of the problems you presently have to deal with? Jot down at least three.

_____

_____

_____

_____

The most obvious constraint is **financial**. Everyone has to work within budgets, and funds are always limited. The next obvious constraint is a **human** one: a solution may require skills that you and your colleagues do not possess. Then there is a question of **authority**: you may see a solution but not have the power to implement it. **Time** is also a consideration. Urgent problems call for quick solutions. Options that take too long are not acceptable.

Physical constraints can also be significant. A work overload problem can perhaps be solved by employing more people, but if there isn't the space to accommodate them, it isn't an option.

Finally – and you may not have thought of this – there may be **cultural** constraints. A solution may be lawful, moral, cheap, timely, physically possible and within your power to implement, but it's still ruled out.

Here's an example of a cultural constraint in operation.

> For a fortnight the weather had been sweltering. Both staff and customers in the shop were complaining. When the temperature became unbearable, the manager told the staff they could wear T-shirts instead of the uniforms specified in the dress code.
>
> The district manager reprimanded the manager on two grounds: first for allowing the dress code to be broken (this was a policy constraint); and second for making the decision without consulting him. The latter was not laid down in any rules or regulations; but the organization's culture was such that no manager was allowed to make a significant decision without referring it upwards first.

Cultural	Lack of authority	Time
Policy	**CONSTRAINTS ON A SOLUTION**	Financial
Moral	Legal	Physical	Human

3.3 What a solution must be

The first part of this session can be summed up like this. A solution to a problem must be:

- **effective:** It must 'cure' the problem either permanently or for a reasonable period of time;

- **efficient:** It must solve the problem without creating lots of extra ones;

- **viable:** It must take account of the various constraints that apply.

What is the distinction between 'effective' and 'efficient'? Suppose you are sitting in an armchair reading the newspaper. You see a fly on the wall. You hate flies. You have two viable solutions: either swat it with the newspaper or throw the armchair at it. Both solutions are **effective** (they both work), but using the newspaper is much more **efficient!**

Activity 42 · 2 mins

If there are only one or two constraints on a solution, you don't necessarily have to abandon it.

Suppose you have a solution that works well in every respect, other than the time it will take to be effective. Perhaps the time constraint is negotiable – that is, when all concerned have had a chance to consider its other merits, they will be prepared to allow it longer to work.

Which of the other constraints would you think are, at least in some cases, negotiable?

Financial	Yes	No
Human	Yes	No
Physical	Yes	No
Legal	Yes	No
Moral	Yes	No
Policy	Yes	No
Cultural	Yes	No
Authority	Yes	No

My personal experience suggests that all of these constraints may be negotiable, except for the legal and moral ones. As with the time constraint, when the solution is basically a good one, you may be able to make a case for more money and human and physical resources.

If you can rally wider support for your solution, you may also be able to overcome policy and cultural constraints, and influence is often an effective substitute for authority.

4 Identify possible solutions

For some problems there is only one solution. For others there may be many possibilities. It makes sense to assemble all the possible solutions before you make your choice. The one that works best may not be the first one that springs to mind, as another look at Bill's problem will illustrate.

In the light of what we now know about its causes, Bill's problem can be restated as follows.

> There is an increase in the number of faulty products which Bill and his team do not have the capacity to handle; this has resulted in stress and demoralization, which are exacerbated by management pressure.

There are three interlocking 'dimensions' here:

- too much work;
- lack of capacity;
- management pressure.

Together, these determine the nature **and the size** of the problem. We can actually show this problem as a three-dimensional shape — a cube, to be precise.

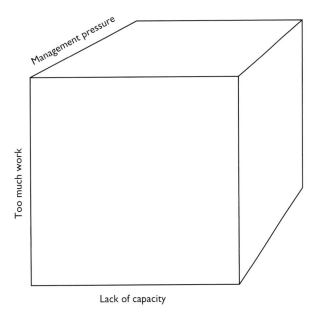

Management pressure

Too much work

Lack of capacity

If the size of any of the three dimensions of the cube can be reduced, the overall size of the problem will be reduced.

Reduce them enough, and the problem disappears!

Activity 43

5 mins

Given the way Bill's problem has been restated and shown as in the figure above, what solutions can you suggest?

_____

_____

_____

_____

_____

_____

Logically, anything that reduces the size of one of the cube's three dimensions will help produce a solution. However, there is a difference between the three causal dimensions that we have identified. **Too much work** and **lack of capacity** are the main factors determining the size of the problem; **management pressure** simply makes it worse. So, while dealing with the management issue will ease the problem, it will not solve it. A solution to Bill's problem has to concentrate on:

- either reducing the number of faults sent for repair;
- or increasing the capacity to repair them.

4.1 Two contrasting approaches

Finding possible solutions is much like finding possible causes. There are basically two different strategies:

- the logical, focused approach;
- the broadly-based, creative approach.

The logical approach

The logical, focused approach is based on the information you have gathered about the problem and the cause(s). Within reason, the more information you have, the better.

You then study the information and make rational deductions about the solution.

Thus in the case of Bill's problem, the solution is clearly one of workload/capacity rather than, say, of Bill's leadership or competence. The problem is not of Bill's making.

Looking at the two main dimensions of the problem, we can say with perfect logic that:

- reducing the number of faulty items being produced will solve the problem;
- increasing the capacity of Bill's team (by offering more overtime work, or employing more people) will solve the problem.

Activity 44

5 mins

We don't know much about the implications of adopting these solutions, but we can be sure that cost is a major consideration.

What comments would you make about the two logical suggestions for a solution?

a   reducing faults

_____

_____

_____

b   increasing capacity

_____

_____

_____

The mention of costs provided you with a strong hint. The company needs to make a profit; if its costs go up, profits will be under pressure. We already know that Bill's manager had ruled out increasing the staff budget, presumably for this reason. Reducing fault levels in Production is easily said but hard to achieve. It may involve operatives working more slowly, more inspection, better equipment, changed methods, etc. All of these also boil down to cost in the end. While making lots of faulty items must reduce profits, the steps needed to reduce the faults may – at least in the short-term – be even more costly.

In practice, there may be many constraints against adopting a seemingly logical solution. We will come back to this issue shortly.

EXTENSION 4
If you are interested in developing your creative skills you might like to take up this extension, or one of the many other writings by 'lateral thinking' expert Edward de Bono. See page 124.

The creative approach

The other option in seeking a solution is to get away from narrow logic and approach the problem from different angles, using 'creative thinking'. This is another situation where a bit of brainstorming may work wonders. If you decide not to use a formal brainstorming session, it is still worth re-examining the problem from different angles.

In Session A Bill's problem was defined from both his point of view and th of the company. However, up to now we've focused on **internal** events th affect the company and its employees – repairs requested by Productic aren't being done quickly enough, Bill's team is overworked, Bill is demora ized – and so on. These are certainly problems, but they are surely not t main concerns for a commercial company.

From a commercial standpoint the main problem is that **customers a complaining**. This presents a major risk to the company: a poor reputatic for quality is easy to get, commercially damaging and exceptionally difficult reverse.

The priority for a solution, seen from this angle, is not to make Productio or Bill, or Bill's team happy, but to make the customers happy.

So here are some suggestions. See what you think.

- There is obviously a quality control problem in Production. Sorting this o will solve the problem cleanly and completely, but it's easier said than don It may take too long, be too costly, and require resources that don't exist the company.
- Why not change the priorities? Why not have Bill's team deal solely wi faults reported by customers, and provide an excellent service in this con mercially sensitive area?
- Faulty items sent for repair by Production could be set aside until there's tim to deal with them – or they could be thrown away.
- Perhaps the solution is to increase Production and live with the fault rate.
- Perhaps a new team within Production could be set up to deal with minc faults there.

Logical reasoning, which is deductive and focused in the Sherlock Holmes tradition, is often referred to as **convergent thinking**. Creative, wide-ranging approaches of the brainstorming type are the opposite: **divergent thinking.**

In general, the best long-term solution would be one that reduced the fau rates in Production, since this ought to be an objective for the company an way. This would reduce customer complaints, and the workload problem would evaporate.

In the short term, the company might prefer a solution that ensured tha faults reported by customers were dealt with promptly. This would give tim to tackle the production quality issue.

Activity 45

20 mins

S/NVQ
C6 or F6

This Activity is the fourth in a series of six which could jointly provide the basis of evidence for your S/NVQ portfolio.

You should now be in a position to start generating possible solutions to the problem you first described in Activity 7. Take some time to do this now. If you have time, try to approach the problem from both the **logical** and the **creative** direction. Using more than one technique will give you different and perhaps contrasting angles on the matter.

Note down your possible solutions, describing them in sufficient detail for you to be able to evaluate them later.

Any work that you do on identifying possible solutions could provide useful evidence of your competence and could be added to your S/NVQ portfolio.

Perhaps you already had some ideas about the possible solution before you began Activity 45. However, when the problem is an important one, it is always worth taking time to examine possible solutions in a systematic way, as we have been doing in this Session.

5 Some solutions are better than others

You will no doubt find that there is often more than one possible – and acceptable – solution to many of the problems that you will encounter. How will you choose between them?

One approach is to use the effectiveness/efficiency/viability checklist on each solution and see which comes out best.

Another approach – and in many ways a better one – is to test the solutio against a set of objectives. These need to be rather more detailed th the 'desired outcome' referred to in Sessions A and B. Objectives are t **specific results** that you wish to achieve in solving the problem.

Of course, there are generally two or three objectives (known as **go/no objectives**) that you **must** achieve in order to be able to say that you ha solved the problem. But there may be others that it would be **desirable**, perhaps just **nice**, to achieve at the same time.

You can in fact think in terms of three levels of objective:

- **must** objectives. If you don't achieve these, you don't have a solution.
- **want** objectives. These are things that it's valuable but not essential achieve;
- **would like** objectives. It would be nice to achieve these, but it doesn't ma ter that much if you don't.

Rhoda has a problem with one of her staff whose work is erratic and who is not always reliable. Her overall 'desired outcome' is either to ensure that this person works to the right standard in future, or to put in motion procedures for replacing him.

Rhoda has worked out three possible solutions – A, B and C. She has then checked them against five specific objectives. If the solution delivers the objective, she gives it a tick.

Objectives	A	B	C
1 **Must** show offender how he can improve his performance	✓	✓	
2 **Must** ensure offender understands what will happen if no improvement	✓	✓	✓
3 **Want** to demonstrate to boss that I am a competent manager		✓	
4 **Want** to demonstrate to team that I can handle such issues fairly	✓	✓	✓
5 **Would like** to teach this person a lesson!	✓		✓
6 **Would like** to have the problem sorted out by mid-July	✓		

Activity 46

Look at Rhoda's checklist above. Which solution is best?

The best solution is: _____

You will find the answer to this Activity on page 131.

5.1 Weighted objectives

There is a more sophisticated way of comparing how different solutions perform in terms of non-essential objectives. Instead of dividing these objectives rigidly into 'wants' and 'would likes', you give each such objective a numerical value, or 'weighting'.

'Weighting' simply means giving a bigger number to things that you value highly, and a smaller number to less important matters. In Rhoda's case the weighting of the four non-essential objectives on her list might look like this.

Non-essential objectives	Weight	A	B	C
3 Demonstrate to boss that I am a competent manager	5		✓	
4 Demonstrate to team that I can handle such issues fairly	10	✓	✓	✓
5 Teach this person a lesson!	2	✓		✓
6 Have the problem sorted out by mid-July	4	✓		
Scores max	21	16	15	12

This method gives a different result: solution A wins by a whisker! Of course, it all depends on what weighting you decide to give each objective. (Remember that solution C is still ruled out because it doesn't deliver both the 'must' objectives.)

Activity 47 · 20 mins

S/NVQ C6 or F6

This Activity is the fifth in a series of six which could jointly provide the basis of evidence for your S/NVQ portfolio.

Draw up your detailed objectives for the problem that you are working on for your assignment. If there are several non-essential objectives, lay them out on the lines shown on page 82.

Now evaluate the potential solutions that you developed in Activity 45 against your objectives.

When you have done this, give your best two or three solutions a further evaluation using the checklist below.

Rate the first two items from 0 to 5.

How effective is it?	0	1	2	3	4	5
How efficient is it?	0	1	2	3	4	5

Is it viable in terms of the following constraints:

Time	Yes	No
Financial	Yes	No
Human	Yes	No
Physical	Yes	No
Legal	Yes	No
Moral	Yes	No
Policy	Yes	No
Cultural	Yes	No
Authority	Yes	No

Where you have identified a constraint, you may find it useful to spell out what this means in practice. The fact that there is a constraint does not necessarily mean that your solution is not viable. You may be able to negotiate your way through it. This is particularly true of financial, human, policy and cultural constraints.

5.2 Check your solutions

When you have identified a small number of solutions – preferably just one or two – that appear to be:

- effective;
- efficient;
- viable;

and seem likely to achieve your desired outcomes and specific objectives, there are a few checks to make.

Ask yourself:

- How easy will it be to implement this solution?

  If you have two good solutions to choose from, the one that is easiest to implement should be your choice.

- What risks are attached to it?

  If you have two good solutions to choose from and one looks less risky than the other, then the one involving less risk should be your choice.

Activity 48 · 3 mins

Here are some pairs of 'risk factors' that might apply to any potential solution to a work-based problem, including the one you have been working on in this workbook.

For each pair, say whether (a) or (b) is the more risky, and why.

1   a   This solution involves installing brand-new state-of-the-art equipment with which we are not familiar.

     b   This solution involves installing extra units of familiar equipment.

       Which is riskier? _____

       Why?   _____

       _____

2   a   The manager has succeeded in working out a solution by himself, without involving his boss or the work team.

     b   Many colleagues have been involved in reaching a decision.

       Which is riskier? _____

       Why?   _____

       _____

3   a   There is plenty of time to implement the solution.

     b   Split-second timing is needed to get the solution on stream in time for it to work.

       Which is riskier? _____

       Why?   _____

       _____

4   a   This is an ingenious but very complex solution.

     b   This is a simple and rather obvious solution.

       Which is riskier? _____

       Why?   _____

       _____

5   a   We are confident that staff and customers will react favourably to this solution.

     b   We are confident about the solution but don't have a clear idea of how staff and customers will react to it.

       Which is riskier? _____

       Why?   _____

       _____

Do you agree that the riskier solutions are (a), (a), (b), (a) and (b) respectively? It should be fairly obvious why, though managers often make obvious mistakes! Whatever the brilliance and attractiveness of a solution, it is always relatively risky:

- to bank on new and untried ideas, equipment or people (1);
- for an individual to work out a solution without consulting and involving others (2);
- to have to work to tight timescales (3);
- to adopt a complex solution (4);
- to proceed without evaluating the impact of a solution on the people it will affect (5).

The risk is of course that the solution will either fail or create unacceptable knock-on problems.

Before you go on to implement a solution, make sure you have a clear understanding of what the risks are. That way, you will have a reasonable chance of being able to minimize them.

6 Decision-making models

6.1 Models

A model is a representation of a real-life thing or situation.

Models allow you to experiment, and try out different scenarios to see which course of action gives the best results. They are used to provide information for decision making when experimenting with real life is impossible, often because it depends on the future and on the actions of others.

There are a number of different sorts of model, such as an architect's miniature model of a building development. The developers will want to see something that gives them an idea of what they will be getting for the millions of pounds they are going to spend, but it would obviously be impracticable and pointlessly expensive to build a full-scale trial version, using genuine materials.

However, in everyday business, decision-making mathematical models are the most commonly used. These represent a real-life situation in terms of mathematical relationships and formulae.

6.2 Examples of business models

Models can be used to help with many kinds of business decision. Here are a number of possibilities.

- **Inventory models**. These help to decide the ideal amounts for stocks of materials or finished goods held, ordering quantities and re-order levels. The EOQ model, a well-known example, follows below.

- **Resource allocation models**. These help the manager to share out scarce resources between competing activities, for example to decide how much time members of the work team should spend on task A, how much on task B, and so on. We'll look at a simple example later in the session. More complex problems need a mathematical technique called **linear programming**, but that is a little too involved for this book. Another approach is to use project management techniques such as **Gantt charts**.

- **Budget models**. These are used to prepare budgets for an organization, such as a cash budget or a breakeven model. Usually you would do this using a spreadsheet (there's an example later in the session), and perhaps some forecasting models.

- **Queuing models**. These simulate arrivals at and departures from a servicing point such as a till in a shop, and show how long the queues will get, depending on how many tills you have open. This can quickly get very complex and a computer is the only way to develop such a model effectively.

- **Business plan models**. These are models used for overall planning by senior managers. Variables would include capital investments, sources of finance, interest rates, assets, liabilities, sales, costs, growth rates, and so on.

There are also modelling techniques that can be used in combination with any of the above, or simply to help you define a problem more clearly. **Probabilities/expected values** and **decision trees** are the best examples, and you'll learn the basics of these techniques before you have finished this session.

6.3 Simple spreadsheet models or 'what if' analysis

Because they generally involve numbers and formulae and logic, many business models are ideally suited for computerization. Complex models will need a specialized computer package, but the familiar spreadsheet can often be used for day-to-day problems.

Once a model has been constructed and saved, the consequences of changes in any of the variables can be tested by asking 'what if' questions (this is also known as 'sensitivity analysis').

For example, a spreadsheet may be used to develop a cash flow model, such as the one below.

	A	B	C	D	E
1			Month 1	Month 2	Month 3
2	Sales	120%	5,000	6,000	7,000
3	Cost of sales	65%	-3,250	-3,900	-4,680
4	Gross profit				
5					
6	**Receipts**				
7	Current month	60%	3,000	3,600	4,320
8	1 month in arrears	40%		2,000	2,400
9	2 months in arrears	0%			0
10			3,000	5,600	6,720
11	**Payments**		-3,250	-3,900	-4,680
12			-250	1,700	2,040
13	Bank balance b/fwd		0	-250	1,450
14	Bank balance c/fwd		-250	1,450	3,490

Here are some typical 'what if' questions.

1   What if the cost of sales is 68% of sales revenue, not 65%?

2   What if payment from debtors is received as follows:

    month of sale   40%

    one month in arrears   50%

    two months in arrears   10%

    instead of 60% in the month of sale and 40% one month in arrears?

3   What if sales growth is only 15% per month instead of 20% per month?

With a spreadsheet model, the answers to questions like these can be found simply and quickly, simply by changing the variables shown as percentages.

The different scenarios give managers a better understanding of what the cash flow position in the future might be, and what they need to do to make sure the cash position remains reasonable. For example, if the company has not agreed an overdraft facility it is going to get into trouble in its very first month! Or it might be found that the cost of sales must remain less than 67% of sales value, or that sales growth of at least 10% per month is essential to achieve a satisfactory cash position.

Activity 49

10 mins

Create a spreadsheet exactly as shown above using formulae wherever appropriate. The only cells that should contain a number are the cells in column B (the variables), cell C2 (5,000) and cell C13 (0). To help you here are the formulae for Month 2.

D
Month 2
=C2*$B$2
=-D2*0.65
=SUM(D2:D3)
=D2*$B$7
=C2*$B$8
=SUM(D7:D9)
=D3
=SUM(D10:D11)
=C14
=SUM(D12:D13)

Once you have done this, save your spreadsheet. Then change the variables and answer the 'what if' questions posed above (what if sales growth is only 15% per month instead of 20% per month). Your answers should state the bank balance at the end of Month 3.

The answers to this Activity can be found on page 132.

6.4 Decision trees

Complex problems need a clear logical approach to make sure that all possible choices and outcomes are taken into account.

Decision trees are a useful way of working through and visualizing such problems.

Decision trees are drawn from left to right, and so a decision tree will start like this.

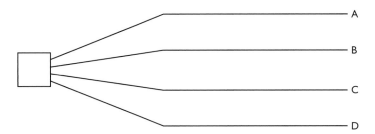

The **square** is the **decision point**, and the 'branches' A, B, C and D are four different choices. For example, your choices might be (A) to use cash to buy new computer equipment; (B) get a loan to buy it; (C) hire the equipment; or (D) continue to use existing equipment.

If a choice can have only one outcome, the branch of the decision tree for that alternative is complete. Usually, though, the choice will have several possible outcomes. We show this on a decision tree by putting in an **outcome point (a circle)** with each possible choice shown as a subsidiary branch.

The probability of each outcome occurring is written on the relevant branch.

In the example above, there are two options facing the decision-maker, A and B. If A is chosen there is only one possible outcome, but if B is chosen, there are two possible outcomes, high profits (0.7 probability) or low profits (0.3 probability).

Activity 50 · 2 mins

In the example above, suppose you are certain that option A will give a profit of £25,000, but you are not sure whether option B will give a profit of £30,000 or £10,000. Which is the best option to choose?

_____

_____

_____

_____

The answer is option A, because option B gives an EV of (£30,000 × 0.7) + (10,000 × 0.3) = £24,000.

In this simple case we didn't really need to draw a diagram, but when there are lots of choices and options decision trees can be very helpful.

For example, sometimes, a decision taken now will mean that other decisions have to be made in the future. Say you have to choose between option A and option B, and depending on the outcome of that decision, you will later have to make a choice between C and D or else a choice between E and F.

If this is the problem you can draw a decision tree like this.

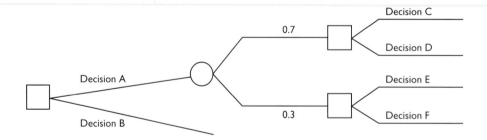

The diagram helps you to visualize and understand this problem much more clearly than the words.

That's enough theory: let's look at a full scale example.

Activity 51

15 mins

Arbor Ltd is considering developing a new product. The company can either test market the product or abandon it.

If the company test markets it, the cost will be £32,000. The market response could be either favourable or unfavourable with probabilities of 0.45 and 0.55.

If the market response is favourable the company could market the product full scale, or they could still abandon the product.

If it markets the new product full scale, the outcome might be low, medium or high demand. The net gains (or losses) would be £64,000, £78,000 or £320,000 respectively and these outcomes have probabilities of 0.21, 0.55 and 0.24 respectively.

If the result of the test marketing is unfavourable but the company goes ahead and markets the product anyway, estimated losses would be £192,000.

If, at any point, the company abandons the product, there would be a net gain of £16,000 from the sale of scrap.

Without looking at our answer see if you can draw a decision tree for the problem faced by Arbor Ltd. Include figures for cost, loss or profit on the appropriate branches of the tree. You might need to try several times, so use a separate sheet of paper for your answer.

The starting point for the tree is to establish what decision has to be made now. The options are:

- to abandon;
- to test market.

The outcome of the abandon option is known for certain: the sale of scrap with a net gain of £16,000.

There are two possible outcomes of the option to test market: favourable response or unfavourable response.

Depending on the outcome of the test marketing, another decision will then be made, to abandon the product or to go ahead.

This is the decision tree.

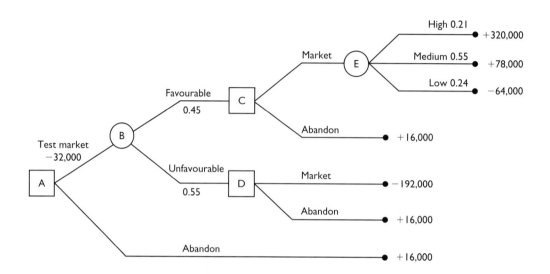

Now we have a nice tree-like diagram, and it helps us to understand the logic of the problem much more clearly. But we still haven't made a decision!

We need to evaluate the tree using expected values. The basic rules are as follows.

We start on the right-hand side of the tree, which represents the future, and work back towards the left-hand side, the decision we have to make now. (This is called the rollback technique.) At each outcome point we calculate the EV.

At **outcome point E** (the right-hand-most point) the EV is as follows.

Sales	£		£
High	320,000	0.24	76,800
Medium	78,000	0.55	42,900
Low	−64,000	0.21	−13,440
			106,260

This is the EV of the decision to market the product if the test shows favourable response. You may like to write the EV on the decision tree itself, at the appropriate outcome point (point E).

At **decision point C**, the choice is as follows.

■ Full-scale marketing EV (the EV at point E) = +£106,260.
■ Abandon = +£16,000.

Obviously the choice would be to market the product, and so the EV at decision point C is **+£106,260**.

At **decision point D**, an unfavourable market reaction, the choice is as follows.

■ Market anyway: loss = −£192,000.
■ Abandon = +£16,000.

Obviously, the choice would be to abandon, and so the EV at decision point D is **+£16,000**.

The later decisions have therefore been made. If the original decision is to test market, the company will market the product if the test shows favourable customer response, and will abandon the product if the test results are unfavourable.

Now we need to calculate the EV at **outcome point B**.

			EV
	£		£
Point C	106,260	0.45	47,817
Point D	16,000	0.55	8,800
			56,617

Finally we compare the options at **decision point A**, which are as follows.

■ Test: EV = EV at B minus test marketing cost = £56,617 − 32,000 = +£24,617
■ Abandon = +£16,000

The choice at decision point A would be to test market the product because it has a higher EV of profit. But there is a lot less in it than you may have thought.

Activity 52

4 mins

In the case of Arbor Ltd (Activity 51) what would the decision have been if the highest probable gains had been £140,000 and the probability of a favourable report had been 0.75?

_____

_____

As you've probably realized, evaluating decisions by using decision trees h
some limitations.

- The outcome with the highest EV may be the riskiest course of action.
- Managers may not be willing to take risks if they may result in losses.
- The probabilities are guesses, and they may well be wrong.

Self-assessment 3 ·

10 mins

1   Postponing a problem won't usually solve it, but it may have one advantag
What is it?

_____

_____

2   There are many constraints that may apply to a solution, but most are
some extent negotiable. Two generally are not. What are they?

_____ constraints

_____ constraints

3   A solution to a problem must be three things, which are spelled out in th
block of letters. What are they?

A	B	C	C	E	E
E	E	E	E	F	F
F	F	I	I	I	I
L	N	T	T	V	V

_____

_____

_____

4   What is 'divergent thinking'?

_____

_____

5   Give an example of a 'creative thinking' technique.

_____

_____

6   At what stage should you evaluate the risks attached to a particular solution?

a When you have identified the cause(s) of a problem.

b When you have set your specific objectives.

c When you have gathered a number of possible solutions but before you select the best one or two options.

d After you have selected the best one or two options but before you make your final choice.

7   A business decision model usually represents a real-life situation in terms of _____. The model will consist of _____. A model allows you to try out _____ to see _____.

Fill in the missing words.

8   Out of 260 working days last year, your work team was one person short through sickness on 23 days. If your work team has 10 members including yourself and everyone works seven hours a day, how many hours' work would you expect to get out of your work team in a typical 22 working day month?

_____

9   Fill in the missing words or phrases below using the appropriate term from the list. You may need to use some terms more than once while you may not use others at all. The terms are:

an outcome point; square; left; circle; a decision point; right

When drawing a decision tree a _____ is used as the symbol for _____, and a _____ is used as the symbol for a decision point. The branches from _____ have probabilities assigned to them. A decision tree is evaluated from _____ to _____.

Answers to these questions can be found on page 127.

7 Summary

- Some 'solutions' are not solutions at all.

  - Postponing a solution doesn't solve it.
  - A bad solution can make matters worse.
  - Some solutions are unacceptable.

- A solution that works must be:

  - **effective**: it will 'cure' the problem either permanently or for a reasonable period of time;
  - **efficient**: it solves the problem without creating lots of extra ones;
  - **viable**: it takes account of the various constraints that apply.

- Possible solutions to a problem can be found by logical deduction or by creative methods such brainstorming.

- The best solutions can be selected by testing them against objectives, which can be thought of terms of three levels:

  - **Must** objectives: if you don't achieve these, you don't have a solution;
  - **Want** objectives: these are things that it's valuable but not essential to achieve;
  - **Would like** objectives: it would be nice to achieve these, but it doesn't matter that much i you don't.

- Non-essential objectives ('musts' and 'would likes') can be weighted to give a more accurate in cation of their importance.

- The final choice of a solution may be made on the basis of which is easiest and least risky implement.

- Managers rarely have all the information they might like, but it is not always worthwhile to obta extra information. The costs should be weighed up against the benefits.

- Models in business are usually mathematical models.

- Decision trees may be used to help define and evaluate complex problems.

Session D
Implementing and evaluating a solution

1 Introduction

Sherlock Holmes was interested in solving problems, but once he had deduced who or what was responsible for the crime, his interest rapidly faded.

He took no part in the tedious business of assembling witnesses, taking statements, bringing the suspect to trial, reaching a verdict, determining a sentence and carrying it out.

In fact you may have noticed that most police and crime dramas also skip this part. In many cases, the villain disappears from the scene in a dramatic manner and there's no need for a trial at all.

However, real life isn't like detective fiction. When you've solved your problem you have to face up to implementing your solution. If you fail at this vital stage, all the effort that went before is wasted.

This session will take you through the two final stages of the problem-solving process: stage five: **implement the solution** and stage six: **monitor and evaluate the solution.**

2 Stage 5: implement the solution

You have by far the best chance of solving a problem when you have:

- thoroughly understood it;
- accurately defined and stated it;
- correctly identified the causes;
- set specific objectives;
- considered the effectiveness, efficiency and viability of your proposed solution(s);
- planned its implementation with care.

But you can still never be completely confident that the solution will work until you have implemented it.

The first point – an obvious one – is that you may need to get other people's **consent** before you can implement a solution. You may need to explain, convince, negotiate.

You may also need their **help** in implementing it. They may control resources, facilities and people without which it can't be done.

You will certainly need to **communicate** with a whole range of other people so that they understand what is happening. **In effect, you need to create an action plan.**

Bill and his manager came up with an effective, efficient and viable solution to Bill's problem that was handled in two stages.

First, new and clear priorities were set.

- Faults reported by customers would be dealt with immediately; Bill was given a small extra budget for overtime to ensure that all such repairs could be carried out within 48 hours.
- Faults reported by Production would in future have to wait until there was time to deal with them; no overtime was allowed for this purpose.

Second, on a longer timescale, the quality problem in Production was to be tackled. It was estimated that it would take up to three months to rectify it.

Activity 53

5 mins

Apart from Bill's own work team, who would need to be told about what was going to happen?

_____

_____

_____

What other actions would Bill have to take to implement this solution?

_____

_____

As illustrated in the diagram below many people will need to be told in the first stage. This will mainly be the responsibility of Bill's manager. He or she will need the approval of higher management for the solution. Production will have to understand the need to give customers priority. Sales and marketing will need to know that service to customers is going to be improved, and they will need to pass this on to customers. Personnel will need to know about the new arrangements for overtime.

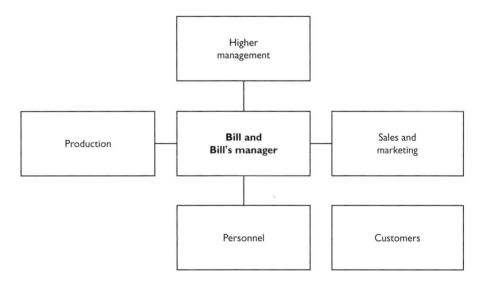

In order to ensure that the new priorities work, Bill will have to establish new systems. He will have to ensure that faulty items returned by customers are repaired within 48 hours. He must therefore log them in and record when they are sent out again. He will need to monitor progress daily, and allocate overtime immediately if it looks as though the standard won't be met.

He must arrange a separate recording system for repairing production faults, and these items must be stored separately.

The second stage of the solution, tackling the quality problem in Production, will be even more complex, and we won't go into that here. (If you want to know more about quality issues, you might like to study another workbook in this series, *Providing Quality to Customer*.)

With so many things to do to put the solution into effect, an action plan will be needed, which states:

- what is to be done;
- start date;
- who is to carry out the action;
- how they are to do it;
- resources required;
- target completion date.

(You will find further details in the Work-based assignment on how to draw up an action plan for implementing a solution.)

2.1 Managing risks and the 'downside'

This is also the stage where you need to think about any risks that you identified in Session C.

When drawing up an action plan, you should make a note of the risks and the action that you need to take to counter them.

 # 3 Stage 6: monitoring and evaluation

Once a problem has been solved, there is a tendency to dismiss it from our minds. Our working life is full of problems, and no sooner do we finish with one problem than we're immersed in the next.

But, as with so many processes, the last stage − in this case monitoring and evaluation − is one of the most important if we are to learn lessons for the future.

3.1 Monitoring progress

It is rarely a good idea to implement a solution and then assume that things will run smoothly without any intervention on our part, especially where big changes are being made to a system or procedure. It is vital to monitor progress for some time after the changes are put into effect and then to evaluate its effectiveness.

Monitoring is the process of checking to find out how well the chosen solution is working. This can be done formally, for example through customer satisfaction questionnaires and computer printouts, or informally, by checking with the people involved to see if their problem has been resolved. You might even try out the improved system for yourself. Situations should be monitored at least until it becomes clear whether or not the solution is effective.

3.2 Evaluation

Evaluation is the process of comparing the actual outcome of the implemented solution (as measured by the monitoring) with your planned outcome, i.e. how successful the solution has turned out to be.

By evaluating your solution as it works in practice, you will achieve three important things:

- You will know whether or not it is working.
- You will see where and how it could be improved.
- You will learn something about how to solve your next problem better, quicker and more efficiently.

Activity 54 · 2 mins

How do you normally judge how well you have solved a problem?

_____

_____

Answering vaguely with something like 'by seeing whether it works' isn't really enough.

There are **four** approaches that you could use.

The first and most obvious one is to go back to the **objectives** that you set for the solution, and ask:

■ How well did it meet my objectives?

The second approach is to refer to **standards**. Many **deviation** problems (where something has gone wrong and needs to be corrected) are standard-based. For example, in the solution to Bill's problem it was decided to adopt a standard of repairing faulty items returned by customers within 48 hours. This is a clear standard, and if it is met, the solution is working, at least to that extent. (As you will realize, a standard may itself form part of an objective.) Thus, you might also ask yourself:

■ Are the required standards being met?

Thirdly, we could judge success in **quantitative** terms – for example, by comparing accident rates before and after implementing a safety improvement.

Activity 55

3 mins

Think of a problem that you've encountered where the effects of a solution can easily be measured in quantitative terms.

_____

_____

You may have suggested a number of things, such as:

■ a problem of increasing productivity (you can compare the numbers produced before and after);
■ a problem of wanting to earn more money (you'll be able to say how much more, if anything, was earned after your solution is implemented than was earned before);
■ a problem of increasing sales (if the solution is a good one, sales will increase by a measurable amount, compared with what they were before).

All these are **improvement** problems. With most improvement problems it is possible to measure and compare solutions in some definite way.

Activity 56

3 mins

Now try to think of a problem where it is more difficult to measure the effects of a solution.

_____

_____

There are plenty of these. Some which come to mind are:

- the problem of trying to improve relations with your boss, or between members of your work team;
- the problem of having to deal with a change of job;
- the problem of re-arranging your office or workshop.

With all these kinds of problem, you may be able to say **whether or not** your solution was successful, but you would find it much harder to say **how well** you've succeeded in solving the problem. This is true of many **potential** problems.

The fourth approach is to look broadly at the 'pros and cons' – the **benefits and drawbacks**. Assuming that a solution has achieved roughly what was intended, you should focus on the downside – the 'cons'. What unwanted side-effects have there been, if any? How many people have been upset, how many orders lost, what additional problems created, what extra costs incurred?

Sometimes the result of applying a solution can have unexpected and unwanted effects. This happens usually when a problem has been defined too narrowly, or insufficient information has been gathered, or the solution has not been thought through in enough detail. The following story is a case in point.

Mike Royce was the supervisor of a DIY and builders' merchants outlet for a firm of timber merchants. In his team were two check-out staff, and five sales staff who dealt with the customers. Mike was overworked, and felt he needed an assistant. He therefore decided to ask Mukesh, a young salesman who seemed the most capable, to help him. He thought he'd better not inform the others about this arrangement, in case anyone got upset.

Mukesh was given a number of tasks, including looking after sales returns, which meant he had to get figures from each of the other sales staff. Within a couple of days, Mike was surprised to find that Mukesh had gone sick, and two of the older sales staff had threatened to walk out.

Activity 57

3 mins

Can you think of a possible reason for this unexpected result?

_____

_____

_____

_____

The reason was that Mukesh had been given no authority to do the job, and his appointment was 'unofficial'. The other sales staff had to learn from Mukesh himself what the new arrangement was, and two of the older ones had got upset about it. They wouldn't co-operate with Mukesh and Mukesh felt he just couldn't cope.

The result would not perhaps have been so unexpected to Mike if he had thought through what he planned to do.

Before applying a solution you need to check that you have thought it through. Once you have applied it, you need to work out its 'downside' – the unwanted effects – and perhaps draw up a balance sheet like the one shown below relating to Bill's problem.

Solution: _prioritize repair of faults reported by customers_	
Benefits	Costs/drawbacks
Customer service improved to standard	Overtime spending greater than hoped
Workload brought to acceptable level	Not able to make any significant impact on backlog of production faults
	Production manager annoyed that his faults aren't being repaired
Overall result: _positive_	

To sum up, evaluating a solution depends on how well you:

■ have identified and defined the problem;
■ are able to assess and measure the situation before a solution is applied;
■ can define attainable and measurable standards;
■ can assess the benefits and drawbacks flowing from the solution.

Implementing a solution can be the hardest stage of all. This isn't the time to 'shut your eyes and hope for the best', though. You will need to apply as much thought and care in putting your plan into effect as you did in developing it.

■ 4 Looking back

Every time you go through the problem-solving process you have the opportunity to learn something that will help you do even better next time.

Let's go through some of the key points to think about when you look back on a problem.

- What caused the problem in the first place? Could it have been avoided?
- Have you taken steps to make sure that the problem won't recur?
- Was your initial approach to the problem the right one? What can be learned from the mistakes made in the early stages?
- Were you objective in your approach to the problem?
- What about the eventual price you had to pay for solving the problem: was it worth it, or would you have been better off not tackling the problem at all?
- Did your definition of the problem turn out to be correct, or were you forced to revise your perception of it?
- Did you have enough information to make a sound decision? Could you have got more?
- Are you confident that you will be able to recognize a problem of the same type in the future, so that you can use a similar solution?
- Can you use the result or method again, for a similar problem?
- Did you use all the help you could get? Were you surprised to find out who the most helpful people were?
- Could you have arrived at the result differently? Does it all now seem obvious?
- Would you tackle a problem like this in the same way again?
- What have you learned?

Activity 58 · 30 mins

S/NVQ
C6 or F6

This Activity is the last in a series of six which could jointly provide the basis of evidence for your S/NVQ portfolio. Whether you can complete it will depend on the exact nature of the problem you have been working on and how quickly and easily your chosen solution can be implemented and evaluated.

When you have had the opportunity to implement your preferred solution, evaluate it against the factors listed in the checklist opposite. The evaluation of how you went about solving your problem could provide useful evidence for your S/NVQ portfolio.

If your evaluation indicates that your solution was a mistaken one, it may not be too late to reverse your decision. If it suggests ways in which the implementation could be improved, you should of course take steps to do this.

In this workbook the examination of problem solving has taken you through six stages:

Stage 1: **recognize** the problem

Stage 2: accept **ownership** of the problem

Stage 3: **understand** the problem

Stage 4: **choose** the best solution

Stage 5: **implement** the solution

Stage 6: **monitor** and **evaluate** the solution.

Self-assessment 4

10 mins

1 Suppose a supervisor boasted to you: 'I had a problem of increasing the output of my work team. I solved it: we are now doing 5 per cent more than last year!'

What would your reaction be? Would you:

a simply congratulate the supervisor for doing a first-class job ☐

b ask what the target had been for increasing output ☐

c ask what other supervisors in the same place of work had achieved by way of increased output? ☐

Briefly explain your choice.

_____

_____

_____

2 Name three ways of evaluating the success of a solution.

_____

_____

_____

3 Which of the following are quantitative measures of success?

a Before the changeover, our performance was poor; now it is considered acceptable. YES   NO

b The target was a productivity improvement of 3.5%. In the event we only achieved 1.75%. YES   NO

c Our main objective was to ensure that Dave was able to operate the new machine to the correct safety standards. This was achieved. YES   NO

d Average call duration had risen to 6 minutes 36 seconds. Following retraining it has fallen to 4 minutes 54 seconds. YES   NO

e We are confident that the improved service for customer repairs will reverse the recent decline in sales. YES   NO

Answers to these questions can be found on pages 127–8.

5 Summary

- In most cases you will need the consent and **help** of other people to implement a solution to a problem.

- You will also need to **communicate** with various interested parties.

- Except in very simple cases, this implies that you will need to draw up an **action plan** showing who will do what, when and how.

- Once you have **implemented** a solution, you should **evaluate** it. This will tell you three things:

  - whether or not it is working;
  - where and how it could be improved;
  - how to solve your next problem better, quicker and more efficiently.

- You can evaluate it in four ways:

  - by comparing the outcome with your original **objectives**;
  - by checking whether any specific **standards** are being met;
  - by making **quantitative** 'before and after' comparisons;
  - by drawing up a balance sheet of **benefits and drawbacks**.

- You should follow up your implementation in two other ways:

  - by **monitoring** the progress of the solution (things seldom go entirely smoothly);
  - by **looking back** over the experience to see what you can learn from it.

Performance checks

1 Quick quiz

Question 1   What should you do before setting out to solve a problem?

_____

Question 2   What is the definition of a problem used in this workbook?

_____

Question 3   There are three main types of problem. What are they?

_____

_____

_____

Question 4   What are the first and last stages in the problem-solving process?

_____

_____

Question 5   What's the value of writing down a problem?

_____

Question 6   In a problem analysis sheet you will be writing down pairs of statements about the problem. What do they tell you?

_____

Question 7   During the brainstorming session, a couple of members of the team repe
edly make suggestions that the rest think are silly, and which aren't writt
down. What is going wrong?

_____

_____

Question 8   What can you gain by doing a fishbone analysis?

_____

_____

Question 9   Collecting more and more information can result in diminishing retur
Why?

_____

_____

Question 10   A school delivers 2,357 pupil-hours of teaching per year. In 2002 if did t
with a staffing level of 15; in 2003 the figure was 14. What were the pu
hours per head for the two years?

2002 _____

2003 _____

Question 11   Why is the arithmetic mean sometimes misleading?

_____

_____

Question 12   How can you estimate an average when you only have grouped data, such
'53 people in the survey were aged between 19 and 25'?

_____

_____

Question 13   If you know the standard deviation of a set of numbers what two things ca
you say about the set of numbers as a whole?

_____

_____

Question 14   Within a long document how should headings and paragraphs be organized

_____

_____

Question 15   What are the key points to remember when presenting numbers in a table?

_____

_____

Question 16   In what sense might a solution be worse than the problem?

_____

_____

Question 17   A solution to a problem must be viable. What is meant by this?

_____

_____

Question 18   Deductive, focused, rational. What is being talked about here?

_____

_____

Question 19   What are the 'go/no go' criteria for a solution to a problem?

_____

_____

Question 20   List three factors that would tend to make a solution relatively more risky.

_____

_____

Answers to these questions can be found on page 132.

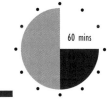

2 Workbook assessment

In every organization there are established procedures and set ways of thinking that persist long after they have ceased to be useful. Managers, supervisors and team leaders often find themselves having to overcome such barriers in the course of dealing with what may be called **improvement problems.**

Let's examine a case in point.

> Bettina has recently been put in charge of the accounts office of a small chain of garages. She is expected to compile a range of data from the branches every week, and finds that many hours of her time are taken up with this. The branch managers are very busy and, although they are always prompt to send in car sales data, most of them have to be reminded time and again to send in the other reports. These include performance data on sales of parts and servicing, labour (hours worked), inquiries handled, discounts and miscellaneous costs.
>
> When Bettina has all the sheets, she has to enter them on the computer, and perform certain calculations. The individual and totalled figures are then passed on to the senior management team, who send a summary to the chairman.
>
> Being new to the job, it occurs to Bettina to ask 'why?'.
>
> ■ Why are the branch managers so reluctant to send in the data, apart from car sales figures?
> ■ Why must the figures be collected once a week? Why not once a month, for example?
> ■ Why does the management team need all this data?
> ■ Why does the chairman need them? What does he do with them?
>
> After asking a lot of questions, she finds out that:
>
> ■ Car sales figures are the overriding priority, perhaps not surprisingly, since this is the main source of revenue for the group.
> ■ There is constant pressure on the branch managers to improve sales. However, branch managers never get any feedback on the other data they have to submit. To them, it's just an irritating chore.
> ■ The management team do use these other data. Actually they enter summaries of Bettina's figures into their own computers. From these they compile four-weekly 'management report', which are useful in various ways. They are not interested in reacting to these data on a weekly basis.
> ■ Once or twice a year, attention turns to these other 'performance measures', and branch managers are called together for a 'gee-up'. No one takes this very seriously, though a manager whose branch performs badly may get a 'grilling'.

Suggest some changes to the system which would achieve the dual objective of reducing Bettina's workload, while still ensuring that all concerned get the information they need.

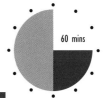

60 mins

3 Work-based assignment

S/NVQs
C6 or F6

The time guide for this assignment gives you an approximate idea of how long it is likely to take you to draft and write up the plan. Your written response to this assignment may provide the basis of appropriate evidence for your S/NVQ portfolio.

What you have to do

Your assignment is to draw up an action plan for implementing the solution to the problem that you have been working on throughout this workbook.

You will need to spend some additional time discussing the issues with colleagues, checking details and thinking about the assignment. The result of your efforts should be presented on separate sheets of paper.

Before you start, look forward to the action plan for your personal development under Reflect and review on page 122. This action plan contains just four column headings:

- Issues
- Action
- Resources
- Target completion date.

What you should write

Action plans vary, depending on their purpose. The plan for implementing a solution to a problem will probably need to include column headings for:

- **action** (state briefly what is to be done);
- **start date**;
- **who is to carry out the action** (for example you, a team member or another colleague);
- **how they are to do it** (this is optional, because although you need to know how, it does not necessarily have to go on the plan);
- **resources required** (money, time, materials, equipment, vehicles, etc.);
- **target completion date**.

It is up to you to decide what column headings you need. You may decide you need extra ones, for example to show **who else is affected** by an action, and **who needs to be kept informed.**

Draw up your implementation action plan in six simple stages.

- **Stage 1** Draft the layout, showing the column headings you intend to use.

- **Stage 2** List all the principal actions needed. Include the communication aspects of the plan, such as announcing it to team and colleagues, and consultation with your line manager.

- **Stage 3** Re-arrange the actions in their logical order. For example, 'Brief staff on new priorities for repairing faulty units' would come before 'Inform customers of new standards for repairs', but after 'Agree solution with higher management'.

- **Stage 4** Decide how long each of the actions in the sequence is going to take (include preparation time – a staff briefing may only take a few minutes, but preparing it can take half a day).

  Bear in mind that two or more actions can often run in parallel, provided that neither depends on the other being completed first. This is a useful way of saving time.

- **Stage 5** Make a final version of the action plan layout. (It is a good idea to make some photocopies before you fill it in.) Fill in the details you have listed above, and add 'target completion' dates.

- **Stage 6** Discuss the final version with your team and colleagues, and modify it if necessary.

  - Does everyone understand what they have to do?
  - Does the timescale make sense?
  - Will the whole process be completed soon enough?

The assignment is to complete and submit a thorough and logical action plan. Of course, if you are dealing with a real problem, you should use your action plan to help you implement your solution. Any notes you add on how well the plan is working may form the basis of evidence for your S/NVQ portfolio.

Reflect and review

1 Reflect and review

This workbook has been all about how to deal with problems in a systematic way. It advises you:

- to hold back and think;
- to step back and analyse;
- to look back and learn.

This obviously isn't necessary for all problems, because sometimes a solution isn't needed, and at other times it's obvious what it must be. But the need for systematic problem solving is undoubtedly real. As Perrin Stryker puts it in his introduction to Kepner and Tregoe's original version of *The New Rational Manager*:

> … the cost of unsystematic and irrational thinking by managers is undeniably enormous. If he wants to, any good manager can easily recall from experience a wide assortment of bungled problems and erroneous decisions. As an executive of a large corporation long honoured for its good management once said to me, 'The number of undisclosed $10,000 mistakes made in this company every day makes me shudder.'

The whole point is that problem solving and decision making needn't be haphazard: these are skills that can be learnt. So let's review what **you** have learnt!

The first objective was:

■ When you have completed this workbook you will be better able to describe and analyse problems.

> ■ This is a matter of systematic thinking and using simple techniques. What new techniques have you learned? In what practical situations have you tried them out?

> _____

> _____

> _____

> _____

The next objective was:

■ When you have completed this workbook you will be better able to identify the cause or causes of problems.

It's amazing how often people look at a problem, and then go straight to proposing a solution without pausing to think about what the problem really is. One repeatedly hears things like 'Sandra's work was not up to scratch, so I gave her a written warning'. A little thought and investigation might have revealed that this was a purely temporary problem, or that there was a medical explanation, or that Sandra needed more training but didn't want to admit it, and so on. Knowing the cause can help us avoid taking actions that might be more damaging than the problem. It can often point us in the direction of a simple and low-cost solution.

> ■ Are you now both ready and able to look at the causes of a problem before jumping to conclusions about the solution? Describe briefly how you now go about this.

> _____

> _____

> _____

> _____

Quite a lot has been said about both logical and creative approaches to discovering causes of problems and to generating possible solutions. It has been recommended that you seek other peoples' advice, and also try to look at the problem from different angles. It is always necessary to challenge your own assumptions, and it is often necessary to challenge existing ideas and ways of doing things in the organization.

Here is the next objective.

■ Understand the need to collect information about problems.

Whenever you are collecting information you should ask yourself questions. Here are some examples.

- ■ Is it accurate?
- ■ Is it relevant?
- ■ Are the sources reliable?
- ■ Does it provide a guide to the future?
- ■ What does it mean?
- ■ How can it be used?

This is partly about understanding information in context, but it is also about being critical. You shouldn't necessarily take things at their face value.

- ■ Think about some information that you have recently received. This might be an unsolicited mail shot, a regular newsletter that you subscribe to or information that you have specifically requested or sought out on the Internet.

- ■ What critical questions could you ask?

_____

_____

_____

The next objective was the first of several relating to the use of information once you have collected it.

The next objectives relate to less routine situations: you have a mass of data, but no predefined way of understanding and summarizing what it all means.

■ Analyse numerical data.
■ Use statistics to enhance understanding of information.

We tried to reassure you that numerical analysis in business frequently involves no more than finding totals and calculating percentages or ratios. Often the question you need to ask is 'what is typical?', and you now know about a selection of averages that you can calculate and the importance of considering the range of the values.

These techniques are valuable in a large variety of operational management situations, for instance when you need to know how the individuals in your team are performing, if you need to set targets, if you want to find out who is the best supplier of a product or service, or if you need to forecast figures, say for budgeting.

■ Think about how you could make more use of simple statistics in your work. Note down some examples of problems that you currently deal with on the basis of 'gut-feeling' or intuition. Would you make better decisions if you took more time to analyse the numbers?

_____

_____

_____

_____

Not all the information you have to deal with is numerical, of course, and this was reflected in our next objective.

■ Analyse qualitative information.

Initial analysis will probably involve sorting the information in some way: by date or by category or alphabetically and so on. And because there is often no 'one best way' of sorting qualitative information it is well worth getting familiar with the sorting facilities that are available in software packages such as Excel with its filters and other tools.

Subsequent analysis of qualitative information, and analysis of information that does not naturally go into a simple list will require report writing skills: how to use a hierarchy of headers, section and paragraph numbering and so on to make it easy for readers to find the information they need at a glance; when (and when not) to include cross-references.

■ Think about some of the reports or other information that you have to generate for others to read. Note down three or four things that you could start doing now to make them work better for your readers.

_____

_____

_____

_____

■ Some of the improvements you would like may involve developing new skills. Make a note of these.

_____

This brings us to the seventh objective:

■ When you have completed this workbook you will be better able to generate a range of possible solutions and decide which will work best.

    ■ How would you now go about generating possible solutions? To what extent have you developed creative thinking skills, especially brainstorming?

    _____

    _____

    _____

    _____

Then we come to the last phases of the problem-solving process. Here there may be a difficulty. After putting lots of energy and brainpower into analysing problems, causes and solutions, you have to implement the best solution, monitor and evaluate it. This may seem the least interesting and rewarding part, but if the solution doesn't work, everything that went before has been a waste of time. A little more effort to ensure the solution is working, and to modify it a bit if necessary, will bring dividends. And last but not least, every problem-solving cycle is potentially a learning experience which can help make you a better manager.

The next objective was:

■ Use decision-making models.

A decision-making model takes some of the pain out of information analysis because it is a tried and trusted technique. You don't have to think too hard about how to analyse the problem, you simply have to plug the numbers into a formula and see what the result is.

There is a wide range of decision-making models – we only looked at a few of the best known ones in this book, particularly stock-related calculations, resource allocation problems and 'what if' scenarios. You may use some kind of model in your work without even realizing it, for example if you or someone else in your department has devised a spreadsheet to quickly calculate the answer to a routine problem, or if you have some kind of specialized software, either part of the accounting system or a stand-alone package.

    ■ What decision-making models do you have to help you with routine decisions that arise in your own work? Have you identified any routine problems that could be dealt with more quickly and effectively if you took the time to develop a spreadsheet solution?

    _____

    _____

    _____

    _____

Our final objective was:

■ When you have completed this workbook you will be better able to implement your chosen solution and evaluate its effectiveness.

■ Are you putting enough effort into implementation, monitoring and evaluation? What more could you do to make your solutions work even better?

_____

_____

_____

_____

2 Action plan

Use this plan to further develop for yourself a course of action you want to take. Make a note in the left-hand column of the issues or problems you want to tackle, and then decide what you intend to do, and make a note in column 2.

The resources you need might include time, materials, information or money. You may need to negotiate for some of them, but they could be something easily acquired, like half an hour of somebody's time, or a chapter of a book. Put whatever you need in column 3. No plan means anything without a timescale, so put a realistic target completion date in column 4.

Finally, describe the outcome you want to achieve as a result of this plan, whether it is for your own benefit or advancement, or a more efficient way of doing things.

Desired outcomes			
1 Issues	2 Action	3 Resources	4 Target completion
Actual outcomes			

3 Extensions

Extension 1

Book *The New Rational Manager:* An Updated Edition for a New World
Authors Charles H. Kepner and Benjamin B. Tregoe
Edition 2002
Publisher Kepner-Tregoe Inc.

This is an updated version of one of the best selling management books of all time. Based on the work of US management consultants Kepner-Tregoe Inc, the book describes in great detail the processes they have developed for solving problems, making decisions, anticipating future problems, and appraising situations. The book uses case studies (one of which is featured in this workbook) all of which illustrate that, no matter how mysterious the problem, they can usually be solved by careful analysis of information.

Extension 2

Book *Managing Information and Statistics*
Authors Roland Bee, Frances Bee
Edition May 1999
Publisher Chartered Institute of Personnel and Development (CIPD)
ISBN 0852927851

Extension 3

Book *Statistics for the Utterly Confused*
Author Lloyd R. Jaisingh
Edition May 2000
Publisher McGraw-Hill
ISBN 0071350055

Extension 4

Book *Lateral Thinking for Management*
Author Edward de Bono
Edition 1990
Publisher Pelican Books (Penguin), London

The well-known author and broadcaster Edward de Bono has made a career from creative thinking. He has written a number of books which advocate the use of a technique he calls 'lateral thinking', as opposed to the application of logic, which he describes as 'vertical thinking'.

4 Answers to self-assessment questions

Self-assessment 1 on pages 35–6

1   The definition should read:

The definition of a problem is: **something which is difficult to deal with or resolve**.

2   Here are the six stages of problem solving correctly completed.

Stage 1:   **recognize** the problem
Stage 2:   accept **ownership** of the problem
Stage 3:   **understand** the problem
Stage 4:   **choose** the best solution
Stage 5:   **implement** the solution
Stage 6:   monitor and **evaluate** the solution

3   The three definitions should read as follows:

a deviation problems are where something has gone wrong, and corrective action is needed.
b potential problems are where problems may be arising for the future and preventive action is needed.
c improvement problems are about how to be more productive, efficient and responsive in the future.

4   The simple test of whether you can define a problem clearly is **whether you can write it down**.

5   The item missing from the list of questions that appear on a problem statement is shown below:

Describe the problem briefly:
What effect is it having?
Where is it?
When was it first noticed?
Is there anything special or distinctive about it?

6   The three 'don'ts' to remember when brainstorming are:

Don't omit any **suggestions**.
Don't **discuss** or **criticize** any suggestions.
Don't try to **sort** the suggestions into **groups**.

7 A fishbone analysis gives you **a complete picture of all the possible causes of a problem**.

8 Rules, procedures, manuals and handbooks can help you solve a problem because they are **concentrated experience in written form**.

Self-assessment 2 on pages 66–7

1 Information is data that has been analysed or processed in some way so as to become meaningful. For instance, data might be organized into a table with column headings and labels.

2 The ratios are as follows.

	Business			
	A	**B**	**C**	**D**
profit	£128,000	£16,250	£3.57 million	£377,500
capital	£605,000	£16,000	£11.5 million	£9 million
ratio:	1:4.73	1:0.98	1:3.22	1:23.84

Business B is the most profitable: it makes a profit of £1 for every 97p invested.

3 In this series of 11 numbers:

- the mean is 62.4/11 = 5.67
- the median is the middle number in the series: 5.4
- the mode is the number that appears most frequently: 5.1.

4
- The upper quartile is the number that 75% of the values in a set of data are less than or equal to.

- The range uses the highest and lowest values from the whole of the data. The inter-quartile range is the difference between the values of the upper and lower quartiles and hence shows the range of values of the middle half of the set of data. So the statement is false.

5 Pivot Tables are useful when there are several different ways to analyse the data, for instance when there are several different categories corresponding to the same figures (for example sales per salesperson per month).

6 By name, by date, by category, in logical sequence and by order of importance.

7 A good understanding of the ideas and information in the documents, and an ability to anticipate the needs of users.

Self-assessment 3 on pages 96–7

1   One advantage of postponing a problem may be that it **gives you more times to find a solution**.

2   The two constraints that are generally not negotiable are **moral** and **legal** constraints.

3   The three things a solution must be, and which you can make out of the block of 24 letters, are **effective**, **efficient** and **viable**.

4   Divergent thinking is a broad, outward-looking and creative approach to ideas.

5   Perhaps the most well-known example of creative (divergent) thinking is brainstorming. Another example is lateral thinking.

6   The correct answer is (d). You should evaluate the risks attached to a particular solution after you have selected the best one or two options but before you make your final choice.

7   A business decision model usually represents a real-life situation in terms of **mathematical relationships and formulae**. The model will consist of **several inter-related variables**. A model allows you to try out **different scenarios** to see **which course of action gives the best results**.

8   The probability of someone being absent is $23/260 = 0.089$. The full number of hours that should be available is $22 \times 7 \times 10 = 1,540$. The expected hours lost are therefore $0.088 \times 1,540 =$ about 136. The expected hours available are $1,540 - 136 = 1,404$. You may have got a slightly different answer, depending on rounding.

9   When drawing a decision tree a **circle** is used as the symbol for **an outcome point**, and a **square** is used as the symbol for a decision point. The branches from **an outcome point** have probabilities assigned to them. A decision tree is evaluated from **right** to left.

Self-assessment 4 on page 109

1   If you simply wanted to be polite, you might choose (a). It would be interesting to know the answers to (b) and (c) though, wouldn't it? If, for example, you learned that all other supervisors had increased output by at least 10 per cent, you might not be so impressed by the boasting supervisor.

2   There are in fact four ways of evaluating the success of a solution to a problem:

   ■ comparing the outcome with your objectives;
   ■ measuring it against standards;
   ■ comparing 'before' and 'after' in quantitative terms;
   ■ drawing up a balance sheet of benefits and costs/drawbacks.

3 Statement (a) is **not** quantitative (it is **qualitative**); statements (b) and (d) **are** clearly quantitative, as they contain numbers. Statement (c) is **not** quantitative, but it is perfectly valid in spite of that. Statement (e) is no more than wishful thinking, and tells us nothing at all about whether the solution has succeeded, either in quantitative terms or otherwise.

5 Answers to activities

Activity 1 on page 7

Try the question on your friends: you'll probably be surprised at how many opt for the £1 million pounds, without a moment's thought.

In fact, option (b) would give you £10,737,418.23 after 30 days!

Unless you do sit down and work it out, though, it is only possible to guess at the answer to this question (unless, of course, you've seen it before). In fact, if option (b) was limited to, say, three weeks instead of a month, you would be far better off with option (a).

Activity 23 on page 41

It would be better if the data were organized in alphabetical order of country, not numerical order. (This would be more obvious if you saw the list with hundreds of codes.)

Activity 24 on pages 42–4

Company	Capital employed (£m)	2004 profit (£)	Capital:profit ratio	Profit %
A	15.80	995,400	1:63,000	6.3%
B	5.90	324,500	1:55,000	5.5%
C	44.20	5,348,200	1:121,000	12.1%
D	21.40	2,461,000	1:115,000	11.5%
E	0.85	79,000	1:92,941	9.3%
F	87.00	13,746,000	1:158,000	15.8%

Most profitable: Company F.

Least profitable: Company B.

**Activity 25
on page 45**

Period	1	2	3	4	5	Average
Data						
Output (units)	217.0	221.0	229.0	214.0	233.0	222.80
Headcount	61.0	61.0	59.0	51.0	51.0	56.60
Cost (£'000s)	119.6	125.3	125.1	119.5	131.3	124.16
Hours worked	2,318.0	2,379.0	2,315.0	2,116.0	2,167.0	2,259.00
Indexes						
Output per head	3.56	3.62	3.88	4.20	4.57	3.97
Cost per unit of output	0.55	0.57	0.55	0.56	0.56	0.56
Hours worked per unit	10.68	10.76	10.11	9.89	9.30	10.15
Cost per head	1.96	2.05	2.12	2.34	2.57	2.21

We have an example here of an organization that is trying to achieve higher productivity, but failing to make real gains.

Productivity, in the form of output per head and the hours needed to produce each unit, has improved considerably. Unfortunately, the labour cost per head has risen, so the cost per unit – the key issue for competitiveness – has remained the same. The aim of improving productivity is to reduce costs in the interests of efficiency and competitiveness. In this example, the wage bill has kept pace with productivity, negating the potential gains.

**Activity 26
on page 46**

Staff	Interviews conducted per day						
	Monday	Tuesday	Wednesday	Thursday	Friday	Total	Average
Dela	45	43	44	21	46	199	39.8
Corinne	54	50	51	55	53	263	52.6
David	38	41	40	44	39	202	40.4

Activity 27
on page 47

Staff	Interviews conducted per day						
	Monday	**Tuesday**	**Wednesday**	**Thursday**	**Friday**	**Total**	**Average**
Dela							
Actual	45.0	43.0	44.0	21.0	46.0	199.0	39.8
Target	52.5	52.5	52.5	52.5	52.5	262.5	52.5
% of target	85.7%	81.9%	83.8%	40.0%	87.6%	n/a	75.8%
Corinne							
Actual	54.0	50.0	51.0	55.0	53.0	263.0	52.6
Target	52.5	52.5	52.5	52.5	52.5	262.5	52.5
% of target	102.9%	95.2%	97.1%	104.8%	101.0%	n/a	100.2%
David							
Actual	38.0	41.0	40.0	44.0	39.0	202.0	40.4
Target	38.0	38.0	38.0	38.0	38.0	190.0	38.0
% of target	100.0%	107.9%	105.3%	115.8%	102.6%	n/a	106.3%

Activity 29
on page 49

	Answer	**Spreadsheet formulae**
Mean	236	= AVERAGE(A1:A9)
Median	249	= MEDIAN(A1:A9)
Mode	263	= MODE(A1:A9)

Not all formulae are as obvious as this, but many are.

Activity 33
on page 60

	A	B	C	D	E	F	G	H	I	J
1							Spring	Summer	Autumn	Winter
2	2000	Spring	5100							
3		Summer	2900							
4		Autumn	7600		=AVERAGE(D5:D6)	=E4/4			=C4-F4	
5		Winter	4600	=SUM(C2:C5)	=AVERAGE(D6:D7)	=E5/4				=C5-F5
6	2001	Spring	5300	=SUM(C3:C6)	=AVERAGE(D7:D8)	=E6/4	=C6-F6			
7		Summer	3600	=SUM(C4:C7)	=AVERAGE(D8:D9)	=E7/4		=C7-F7		
8		Autumn	7500	=SUM(C5:C8)	=AVERAGE(D9:D10)	=E8/4			=C8-F8	
9		Winter	4300	=SUM(C6:C9)	=AVERAGE(D10:D11)	=E9/4				=C9-F9
10	2002	Spring	4900	=SUM(C7:C10)	=AVERAGE(D11:D12)	=E10/4	=C10-F10			
11		Summer	3900	=SUM(C8:C11)	=AVERAGE(D12:D13)	=E11/4		=C11-F11		
12		Autumn	7800	=SUM(C9:C12)	=AVERAGE(D13:D14)	=E12/4			=C12-F12	
13		Winter	5200	=SUM(C10:C13)	=AVERAGE(D14:D15)	=E13/4				=C13-F13
14	2003	Spring	5400	=SUM(C11:C14)	=AVERAGE(D15:D16)	=E14/4	=C14-F14			
15		Summer	3800	=SUM(C12:C15)	=AVERAGE(D16:D17)	=E15/4		=C15-F15		
16		Autumn	8500	=SUM(C13:C16)						
17		Winter	4900	=SUM(C14:C17)						
18							=SUM(G2:G17)	=SUM(H2:H17)	=SUM(I2:I17)	=SUM(J2:J17)
19										
20							=AVERAGE(G2:G17)	=AVERAGE(H2:H17)	=AVERAGE(I2:I17)	=AVERAGE(J2:J17)
21	2004	Total	23000				=$C$21/4	=$C$21/4	=$C$21/4	=$C$21/4
22							=SUM(G20:G21)	=SUM(H20:H21)	=SUM(I20:I21)	=SUM(J20:J21)
23										
24										
25										

If sales demand is 28,000 units the sales pattern will be as follows.

Spring	Summer	Autumn	Winter
6,837.5	5,354.17	9,395.83	6,412.5

Activity 34
on pages 61–2

The information is organized in ascending order of employee number.

It could be organized in alphabetical order of last name or first name, by position, in chronological order of date joined, or (if the dates in the last column are recognized as dates) according to date of 2004 Annual Review. The best way to organize the data is probably by last name. Arguably it could be organized by date of Annual Review, since this would highlight the fact that some reviews are overdue and action is needed.

Activity 36
on page 64

Cross-references to paragraph numbers involve less work and carry less risk of error. When you add material to a document, or delete material, all the subsequent page numbers are likely to change, so if you cross-refer to page numbers you will have to revise all the cross-references that appear after the insertion or deletion. If you cross-refer to paragraph numbers, however, only a few references will change if you delete something or insert something new.

Activity 46
on page 83

The 'musts' are the minimum objectives. They are **'go/no go criteria'**: any solution that does not deliver them is 'no-go'. That rules out Option C, because it does not show the offender how he can improve his performance.

The choice is therefore between Options A and B, which both deliver the minimum objectives. The best choice appears to be B, because it also delivers **both** of the 'want' objectives, which are the next most important. Option A delivers one 'want', plus both the 'would like' objectives, but this still puts it below Option B in rank order.

Activity 49 on page 90

Here are all the formulae. To see yours like this press **Control + `** (the key just above the Tab key) and to get the numbers back again press **Control + `** again. You may want to print it out in formula form, to show that you have done this Activity, and print out the numbers versions when you are doing the 'what if' analysis.

	A	B	C	D	E
1			Month 1	Month 2	Month 3
2	Sales	1.2	5000	=C2*$B$2	=D2*$B$2
3	Cost of sales	0.65	=-C2*$B$3	=-D2*$B$3	=-E2*$B$3
4	Gross profit		=SUM(C2:C3)	=SUM(D2:D3)	=SUM(E2:E3)
5					
6	**Receipts**				
7	Current month	0.6	=C2*$B$7	=D2*$B$7	=E2*$B$7
8	1 month in arrears	0.4		=C2*$B$8	=D2*$B$8
9	2 months in arrears	0			=C2*$B$9
10			=SUM(C7:C9)	=SUM(D7:D9)	=SUM(E7:E9)
11	**Payments**		=C3	=D3	=E3
12			=SUM(C10:C11)	=SUM(D10:D11)	=SUM(E10:E11)
13	Bank balance b/fwd		0	=C14	=D14
14	Bank balance c/fwd		=SUM(C12:C13)	=SUM(D12:D13)	=SUM(E12:E13)

If the cost of sales is 68%, the bank balance at the end of Month 3 is £2,944. Remember to change the figure back to 65% before doing the next part.

If the payment pattern changes, the bank balance at the end of Month 3 will be £1,450. Again, remember to restore the original figures.

If sales growth is only 15%, the bank balance at the end of Month 3 will be £3,432.

6 Answers to the quick quiz

Answer 1   Before setting out to solve a problem you should **think about it**.

Answer 2   A problem is **something that is difficult to deal with or resolve**.

Answer 3   The three main types of problems are **deviation, potential** and **improvement** problems.

Answer 4   The first stage in the problem-solving process is to **recognize the problem**. The last is to **evaluate the solution**.

Answer 5   Writing down a problem helps you clarify the details in your mind, and sometimes even suggests a solution right away.

Answer 6   The pairs of statements in a problem analysis sheet tell you what the problem **is**, and what it **could be, but is not**.

Answer 7   In brainstorming, all suggestions should be noted down, and no one should be made to feel that their ideas are silly.

Answer 8   A fishbone analysis should give you a complete visual picture of the possible causes of a problem.

Answer 9   Collecting more and more information can result in diminishing returns because the cost of collection and the time needed to process and interpret the information begin to outweigh its extra value.

Answer 10   In 2002 the ratio was approximately 1:157. In 2003 it was approximately 1:168.

Answer 11   The mean can easily be distorted by the inclusion of one or more untypical figures, in other words a figure much higher or lower than the majority of the values.

Answer 12   To calculate the average when you have grouped data, you need to decide which value best represents all of the values in a particular class interval. It is a convention in statistics to take the mid-point of each class interval, on the assumption that the frequencies occur pretty evenly. In this example the mid-point is 22.

Answer 13   ■ Sixty-eight per cent of the values in a set of numbers will be within plus or minus **one standard deviation** of the arithmetic mean.
   ■ Ninety-five per cent of the values in a set of numbers will be within plus or minus **two standard deviations** of the mean.

Answer 14   There should be a 'hierarchy' of headings: an overall title, section headings and within each section up to three levels of sub-heading. Sections might be lettered A, B and so on; main points numbered 1, 2, and so on, paragraphs numbered 1.1, 1.2, 2.1, 2.2; and sub-paragraphs 1.2.1, and so on.

Answer 15   Numbers should be right-aligned and they are easier to read if you use the comma separator for thousands. Decimal points should line up, either by using a decimal tab or by adding extra zeros. A total figure is often advisable at the bottom of each column of figures and possibly at the end of each row.

Answer 16   A solution might be worse than the problem if it causes more or worse problems than there were to begin with.

Answer 17   A viable solution is one that works while also taking account of the various constraints that apply.

Answer 18   **Deductive, focused** and **rational** are words that describe the logical, as opposed to the creative, approach to finding possible causes of and solutions to a problem.

Answer 19   The 'go/no go' criteria are the objectives that a solution must deliver if it is to be considered a success.

Answer 20   Risk factors for a solution include:

- relying on new or untried ideas, equipment and people;
- failing to consult and involve others;
- tight timescales;
- complexity;
- failure to evaluate the impact that the solution will have on the people it affects.

7 Certificate

Completion of this certificate by an authorized person shows that you have worked through all the parts of this workbook and satisfactorily completed the assessments. The certificate provides a record of what you have done that may be used for exemptions or as evidence of prior learning against other nationally certificated qualifications.

superseries

Solving Problems and
Making Decisions

....

has satisfactorily completed this workbook

Name of signatory ....

Position ....

Signature ....

Date ....

Official stamp

Pergamon
Flexible
Learning

Fifth Edition

superseries

FIFTH EDITION

Workbooks in the series:

For prices and availability please telephone our order helpline
or email

+44 (0) 1865 474010

directorders@elsevier.com

Published by Scholastic Inc.
90 Old Sherman Turnpike, Danbury, Connecticut 06816.

For information regarding permission, write to:
Disney Licensed Publishing
114 Fifth Avenue, New York, New York 10011.

ISBN 0-7172-6810-1

Designed and produced by Bill SMITH STUDIO.

Printed in the U.S.A.
First printing, December 2003

On with the Show!

A Story About
Creativity

by **Joanne Barkan**
illustrated by
S.I. International

SCHOLASTIC INC.

New York   Toronto   London   Auckland   Sydney
Mexico City   New Delhi   Hong Kong   Buenos Aires

"*A*h, breakfast was *magnifique!*" Lumiere said to Mrs. Potts. He started to gather up his dirty dishes but stopped. "You know, this silverware looks dull. I will have it polished today."

A few minutes later, Lumiere had the Polishing Cloths hard at work in the dining room.

"*T*en o'clock!" Cogsworth muttered as he hurried into the dining room. "Time to count—"

Cogsworth stopped short when he saw what the Polishing Cloths were doing and gasped. "May I ask *what* is going on in here?"

"*L*umiere told us to polish the silver," one of the Cloths answered.

Cogsworth frowned. "I did not plan to have you polish silver. And I give the orders here!"

With that, he stomped off to find Lumiere.

Cogsworth found Lumiere in the library, helping Featherduster.

"Lumiere," Cogsworth said, "it was my intention to have the Cloths clean the ballroom chandelier, but you have them polishing silver."

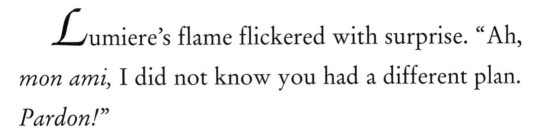

*L*umiere's flame flickered with surprise. "Ah, *mon ami*, I did not know you had a different plan. *Pardon!*"

Cogsworth turned to leave the room. "Do keep in mind that I am the head of the household."

*L*umiere followed Cogsworth into the hall. "*I* am head of the kitchen and dining room," Lumiere said. "I'm more important!"

"No, *I* am more important," Cogsworth answered haughtily.

"Why, you . . . you overgrown pocketwatch!" Lumiere retorted.

"You wax-headed wick brain!" cried Cogsworth.

Lumiere swept into the kitchen, flaming. "If that Cogsworth is so important, he can run the castle himself," he said to Mrs. Potts. "I will not speak to him until I get a full apology."

With that, he planted himself on a tall stool.

*C*ogsworth marched into the library, ticking louder than ever and muttering to himself. "If Lumiere is so important, he can run this place himself! I will not speak to him or leave here until he apologizes."

With that, he plunked himself down on the mantle.

All that day, everyone in the castle tried to help end the quarrel.

Finally, Belle went to see Cogsworth. "You and Lumiere are equally important," she explained. "We need both of you to run this castle well."

Later, she said the same thing to Lumiere.

"*A*re you going to sit there until you gather cobwebs?" Featherduster asked Cogsworth. "Think of all the orders you could be giving."

"I guess you won't be needing these any longer," Chip later said to Lumiere with a sigh. He put Lumiere's extra candles into a drawer.

A week went by. Everyone was glum. They missed Lumiere swishing up and down the stairs and Cogsworth ticking in and out of every room.

"How did the Beast end these squabbles before I arrived?" Belle asked Mrs. Potts.

"*H*e would lose his terrible temper," Mrs. Potts said. "He frightened everyone into obeying."

"There must be another way," Belle sighed. "Maybe a walk in the garden will help me think."

"*I*f only Cogsworth and Lumiere could see that we need them both," she thought. "If only we could show them how foolishly they're acting." *What would a princess do?*

*B*elle sat down and stared at the water splashing in the fountain. "Yes, show them how they're acting. . . . "

"That's it!" she said, jumping up. "We'll put on a play!"

*B*elle called a secret meeting. Everyone except for Cogsworth and Lumiere met in the dining room. Belle described her plan.

When she was finished, the Beast said, "Putting on a play is a great idea, Belle. But the rest of us have never done it before."

"Neither have I," Belle said. "We'll have to be creative. That means we'll use our imaginations. Each of us has special talents to use, too."

"Yes, I'll do the costumes," Wardrobe said.

"Nails and I can build the sets," said Hammer.

The ideas began flying back and forth. Within an hour, the friends had come up with story suggestions, costume sketches, and plans for the scenery.

"So far, so good," Belle said. "Now it's time to turn our ideas into a real play."

*H*ammer and Nails got to work building a stage in the ballroom. Featherduster painted the scenery.

Wardrobe and Mrs. Potts began sewing costumes. Belle and the Beast wrote the script. Chip ran back and forth, delivering messages.

The harder they worked on the play, the better everyone felt. As their spirits rose, they became more hopeful about ending the argument.

Meanwhile, Cogsworth and Lumiere sensed that something strange was going on. But no one said a word to them about the secret play.

$\mathcal{T}$he big night arrived. Belle persuaded both Lumiere and Cogsworth to come to the ballroom for one hour.

"Who gave permission to build a stage in the ballroom?" Cogsworth asked as he sat down.

"*What* is going on here?" Lumiere muttered.

The lights dimmed. Violin and Piano struck up a tune. The curtain opened slightly, and the Beast stepped out.

"*L*ong ago, Sun and Rain argued," the Beast announced just before he opened the curtain wide.

"Without me," Sun claimed, "the crops will not grow and the flowers will not bloom."

"Without me, all the plants will dry up and die," said Rain. "So *I'm* more important!"

"*N*o, *I'm* more important!" declared Sun.

"If you're so important, then you can do all the work yourself!" Rain answered.

"No, you can do all the work!" Sun said.

Sun refused to shine, and Rain refused to fall. The flowers faded and the crops withered.

One day, a seedling went to see Sun and Rain. "I'm just a few weeks old," he said, "but I know that I need *both* Sun and Rain to grow."

Just then Spring appeared. "That's one smart seedling," she said.

Sun and Rain looked at each other and
nodded. Rain scattered some clouds across the sky
and began to fall. Sun shone between the clouds.

As Spring raised her rainbow, the seedling
began to grow.

The curtain closed. The audience clapped and cheered.

"Bravo!" Lumiere shouted, peeking at Cogsworth out of the corner of his eye.

"Good show!" Cogsworth called out, glancing at Lumiere.

$\mathcal{B}$elle was watching them. "So you liked the play?" she asked as she drew them together.

"*Oui, oui*," Lumiere said. "It was very . . ."

"Yes," Cogsworth began, "it was very . . ."

Belle smiled. "True to life?" she suggested.

"*H*opefully, we'll have *two* happy endings, today," Belle hinted to her friends.

Looking at Lumiere, Cogsworth asked, "Friends?"

"Ah, *mon ami*," Lumiere said, "of course."

They walked off, side by side.

"The play was the perfect answer, Belle," the Beast said. "In fact, we all liked working on it so much, maybe we should do another."

"Next time, let's do it *before* anyone quarrels," Belle laughed. "Now, wouldn't that be creative?"

The End